FRANK LLOYD WRIGHT

HIS LIFE □ HIS WORK □ HIS WORDS

FRANK LLOYD WRIGHT

HIS LIFE □ HIS WORK □ HIS WORDS

BY OLGIVANNA LLOYD WRIGHT

LONDON □ PITMAN PUBLISHING □

First published in Great Britain 1970

Sir Isaac Pitman and Sons Ltd.
Pitman House, Parker Street, Kingsway, London, W.C.2
P.O. Box 6038, Portal Street, Nairobi, Kenya

Sir Isaac Pitman (Aust.) Pty. Ltd.
Pitman House, Bouverie Street, Carlton, Victoria 3053, Australia

Pitman Publishing Company S.A. Ltd.
P.O. Box 9898, Johannesburg, S. Africa

ISBN: 0 273 31469 6
GO—(G. 3359)

PICTURE CREDITS

John Amarantides: page 25 (bottom), 83, 93, 96 (left and right), 97 (left and right), 101, 105 (bottom), 106, 107, 176, 177

Doug Brader: 199

P. E. Guerrero: 175

Hedrich-Blessing: 76, 77, 128, 129

Ch. Hirayama: 69

W. Albert Martin: 55 (bottom)

Robert E. Mates: 163

Dorothy M. McKinney: 164

Herb McLaughlin: 192

Richard Nickel: 36, 52

Obma Studio: 15 (left and right)

Roy E. Petersen: 119

Joe D. Price: 117

Reierson Studio: frontispiece

Karl H. Reik: 190-91

Royal Photo Co.: 197

William H. Short: 168

Ezra Stoller: 160, 165

Vernon Swaback: 154, 155, 156, 157

William Wollin Studio: 198

Tom Woodward: 25 (right)

CONTENTS

INDEX TO ILLUSTRATIONS

THE FIRST YEARS

Frank Lloyd Wright was born in Richland Center, Wisconsin, a small town in a countryside studded with meadows and cliffs and smooth, soft, wooded hills. He told me that he had made his entrance into the world on a stormy night and described it to me as though he had witnessed the prophetic initiation. The wind rose over the earth forcing trees low to the ground. Lightning ignited the clouds and thunder struck like a giant in fierce fury. The elements shook the little house which stood up bravely against the attack. "Yours was a prophetic birth," his mother told him.

"It goes to show that nature made her most dramatic display in greeting me on June 8th, 1869," he liked to say.

His mother believed that his birthday marked the nature of his life; and his life unfolded in the midst of drama, tragedy, struggle, beauty, heroism.

The influences in the first years of his childhood affected his future forcefully. Through his Welsh ancestors Frank Lloyd Wright from the very beginning of his life was subject to a great variety of experiences. His grandfather, Richard Lloyd Jones, a strong-spirited Unitarian, had come from Wales with his family to found a new community in the green-hilled valley near Spring Green, Wisconsin. His five uncles be-

came men of influence. Jenkin Lloyd Jones, a Unitarian minister, was
well known in Chicago for his fine sermons and an electrifying per-
sonality. The four other brothers stayed in the valley as successful
farmers, all handsome and impressive men commanding instantaneous
respect wherever they went. His tall, aristocratic-looking mother and
aunts reached prominence in the field of education by founding one
of the first coeducational home-schools in the country.

As a child Frank Lloyd Wright had constant communication with
those Welsh relatives who resembled Shakespearean characters; they
all retained the power of their Druid bloodlines and possessed an intuitive sense of drama, with slashing tempers and dark tumultuous na-
tures, but with it all went an abundant laughter. I used to tease him,
reminding him that his remote ancestors had committed human sacrifices on the huge, vertical Speaking Rocks in Wales. The power of those
characters was imprinted upon him. They were cut of granite.

GRANDMOTHER AND GRANDFATHER RICHARD LLOYD JONES

It is important that a child should not be entirely submerged in trivialities when this most valuable time of all can be spent to great advantage; in the first years of his childhood, he lived in a stern and disciplined household where there was little trivial talk. His mother was a woman of regal character who sometimes inspired fear and who knew exactly what she wanted her son to be; she worshipped him. She loved her two daughters, but into her cherished son she poured all her own unfulfilled desires. Anna Lloyd Wright was a woman in advance of her time. Though she saw ahead of the era in which she lived, she could not give her vision much form besides hanging straight curtains in her house—at that time almost a revolutionary act since curtains were traditionally looped and pulled apart by a ribbon—and she could invent color schemes with her own original flair. She passionately desired a higher self-expression which, in the social conditions of the time, was impossible for a woman to achieve, so she put all her aspirations, her pent-up energy, into her son, daily developing in him a sense of the relationship of nature, religion and philosophy to man. Her Welsh blood, filled with the spirit of ballads, legends and songs of Taliesin, the Welsh bard, flowed fast through her son's being. It was not by way of education that he received his intellectual development; he received it by way of his heritage. It was "blood knowledge," such as streamed through the veins of his Druid-Welsh ancestors.

F.LL.W. AT TWO-AND-A-HALF

His mother, intent upon the perfect growth of her son, kept injecting him with ideas of a world that would be far greater than the one in which she lived. She wanted above all to see him create in a world of vision. That is why she had hung architectural gravures in his room, why she had brought him the Froebel kindergarten blocks to play with when he was seven and why she sought in every form and fashion to give him more than an ordinary school could give him. She educated him herself and in that intimate contact she was able to impart to her son many a treasure which is missed under ordinary conditions, where too often parents, teachers and educators accept and carry on ready-made formulas. She created freshly for him and he held his mother in immeasurable veneration all his life. I know of no other genius who possessed such reverence for his mother. Eighty years later, in his book *A Testament*, he was to write in gratitude for her gifts of the Froebel cardboard triangles and maple-wood blocks: "All are in my fingers to this day."

ANNA LLOYD WRIGHT

WILLIAM CARY RUSSELL WRIGHT

His father, William Cary Wright, was a Yorkshireman, who was a talented musician. His little boy admired him but it hurt, he used to recall to me, to see the face of his father smeared with ink spots, ink all over his hands, even on his teeth, when he was at work on compositions. Music occupied much of the child's life, although he resented listening to Beethoven's sonatas played late at night when, as a tired little boy, he wanted only to sleep. He resisted it then as he resisted the oatmeal which his mother forced him to eat at breakfast each day. In fact, though he began by hating oatmeal, that custom too became part of him. This apparently superficial thing became as fundamental to him as breathing, and in later life, every morning without fail, he insisted on having his bowl of oatmeal no matter where we were, till his last days on earth. It was the same with music which was given to him in such big doses in childhood that a passionate love of music developed in him without which he could not live.

Although William Cary Wright exerted a permanent influence on his son's life, it was his mother who affected the development of spirit in him and the gift to perceive the interior world in everything he saw.

She loved to pick wildflowers in the hills and meadows, studying them, arranging them in clusters, explaining to him the intricate formations of petals in relation to leaves and stem. She loved ferns because of their geometric design and passed that love to her son, so that today the walks and gardens of our home in Taliesin, Wisconsin, are everywhere filled with ferns. Whenever he and I walked through the woods, the first thing we did was to dig up some wild ferns to take home. He would remember and repeat to me his mother's words, "See, what a lovely design is in these leaves. Have you ever imagined that nature could mold such a form? Study nature, love nature, stay close to nature, my son, it will never fail you." That was in her blood, the inspiration and essence of her life with which she electrified her son, and her love was healing to him at the worst times of his life.

Of all his uncles, he worshipped James Lloyd Jones and "wanted to be just like Uncle James"—handsome, compelling, outspoken—and as a youth he even tried to imitate this Welsh patriarch. But all the uncles

UNCLE ENOS

UNCLE JENKIN

UNCLE JAMES

were irrepressible, with their own ideas as to the universal order of things. With dark shocks of hair and thick beards they were often referred to as "prophets" or "apostles" and each of them in some way influenced the nature of the young genius. Jenkin Lloyd Jones, the minister who built the first Unitarian Church in Chicago, was poetic and forceful, a magnetic speaker. While listening to his uncle's sermons in childhood, the boy was exhilarated by the fiery words. Continually exposed to well-correlated people, articulate of speech, coordinated in their work, with a sense of drama ever present, he grew up in an environment where the earth was respected and loved, and among people who thrived on hardship—all reminiscent to me of my own Montenegrin background. Once, looking at portraits of my ancestors on a big plaque, he remarked with delight, "Did you notice? They all look Welsh! There isn't one of them that doesn't have the proud, volcanic look of a Welshman." He frequently mentioned that, because his father was a Yorkshireman, he also had English blood in him, but that was secondary; he was very proud of being Welsh.

Although fundamentally an American, he paid homage to that ancestry. We travelled to Wales in 1956 when he was invited to come and receive honors as one of their sons. He was as gay and happy as a young boy to be there in that wildly picturesque country. We walked on many roads and through the fine gardens and once, when we came across an old cemetery, we looked for some of his ancestors' graves. We tried to read those complex Welsh names which were almost impossible to pronounce, even for him, though he did not want to admit it: Evrawc, Manawyddan, Wledig, Llevelys, Fflwch. At last we found one tombstone with the name WRIAETH inscribed on it. He was overjoyed. He walked all around it, then "a vague sense of belonging here comes over me," he said. "Let us go on."

Driving through the mountains near the sea, we stopped, leaving the car to walk up a steep, rocky hillside bejewelled with springs and waterfalls, and looked at gigantic trees stretched across the sky. He pointed to one: "This one is mighty enough to hold Merlin, King Arthur's magician, who was turned into a tree by a Welsh sorceress." Near the sloping, sinuous roots we gathered small bunches of wild flowers. I felt my husband was somewhat disappointed that the Welsh had become a civilized people, no longer believing in talking stones and no longer committing human sacrifices!

With such an inborn, sentimental feeling for the country of his ancestors, he was greatly pleased to receive the official honor from the president of the Welsh University at Bangor. He kept reminiscing to me, tracing his memories back to his grandfather and grandmother who had come out of this poetic environment. "I can now understand," he said, "the greatness that my uncles and aunts possessed." His two aunts were educators; very advanced for their time, they had founded the Hillside Home School in Wisconsin, a coeducational endeavor, and had achieved for it a fine academic standing.

AUNT NELL, AUNT JANE, MOTHER

During his early childhood, the family moved to Boston, where they lived for three years, but his mother soon realized that the city environment was not for her son. She was afraid he was becoming too detached, dreamy, perhaps too sensitive. They returned to Wisconsin, where she was convinced that if she now gave him earth under his feet and a plow in his hands, hard work would connect him in concrete terms with his plentiful imagination. She sent him to the Wisconsin farm of his beloved Uncle James in the spring, when snow still covered the ground.

TEN YEARS OLD

Farm life was very rough on a boy of eleven. My husband often told me that he could never forget being roused from sleep by his uncle at four o'clock every morning. Uncle James would rap on the stovepipe that went from the kitchen up to the boy's room, to wake him in the bitter cold mornings, and he began to experience hardships he had never before known in his young life. He used to cry, he said, up there in that attic room on the farm lonely and white with snow, feeling that his mother had deserted him. He cried getting dressed and he cried before going downstairs where, before his Welsh uncle, he had to show himself to be a man.

The adjustment to that life was long and hard, and several times he tried to run away, but was brought back again to face the same hardships. As time went on he began to accept this harsh share. He exerted a supreme effort to fulfill what was demanded of him and thus was able to find in that life things that interested him. He discovered flowers of infinite variety, vari-colored sand on the banks of the river, springs concealed in the hills. How many times in later years we drove on his favorite road near Taliesin and, just before the road ran up a steep hill, he spoke off and on, through all those years of our rides together, about the stratified sand with which he had once "designed buildings."

"Can you see me there, Olgivanna, a curly-headed boy, all alone, sculpting, playing in the sand, constructing a building with branches and rocks, then planting grass around it, making a little garden of flowers—can you see me there?"

"Yes, I can see you. And now you are 'playing' with the same sand, the same rocks, the same flowers, but you have added glass and steel, concrete, brick and wood."

At the age of sixteen, after having gone to the Second Ward School and then to the Madison High School, graduating at fifteen, he attended classes in engineering with Allen Conover, Dean of Engineering at the University of Wisconsin, who had a private practice of his own in Madison. Anna Lloyd Wright, anxious to fulfill the dream of a future in architecture for her son, arranged for him to work in Mr. Conover's office afternoons so that he could attend morning classes and study in the evenings.

It was about this time that the boy witnessed a tragic accident which, as he described it many years later, "had its effect upon the incipient architect all his life long.

"Passing by the new North-wing of the old State Capitol, he was 'just in time' to hear the indescribable roar of building collapse and see the cloud of white lime dust blown from the windows of the outside walls, the dust-cloud rising high into the summer air carrying agonized human cries with it. The white dust-cloud came down to settle white over the trees and grass of the park. Whitened by lime dust, as sculpture is white, men with bloody faces came plunging wildly out of the basement entrance blindly striking out about their heads with their arms, still fighting off masonry and beams. Some fell dead on the grass under the clear sky and others fell insensible. One workman, lime-whitened, too, hung head-downward from a fifth-story window, pinned to the sill by an ironbeam on a crushed foot, moaning the whole time.

"A ghastly red stream ran from him down the stone wall.

"Firemen came soon. Crowds appeared as though out of the ground and men frantically tugged and pulled away at the senseless mass of brick and beams to reach the moans for help of the workmen lying dying beneath them. White-faced women, silently crying, went about looking for husbands, brothers or sons.

"A sudden movement of alarm and scattering of the crowd startled him, as someone pointed to a hand sticking out between chunks of brick-work on which the crowd itself was standing. After pulling away bricks and finally scarlet plaster, a mangled human being was drawn out—too late. One of the sobbing women knelt over it on the grass. And so it went all day long and far into the night.

"The youth stayed for hours clinging to the iron fence that surrounded the park, too sick with the horror of it all to go away. Then he went home—ill. Dreamed of it that night and the next and the next. The horror of the scene has never entirely left his consciousness and remains to prompt him to this day.

"Only outside walls were left standing. The interior columns had fallen and the whole interior construction was a gigantic rubbish-heap in the basement.

"The huge concrete piers in that basement, on which rested the interior cast-iron columns supporting the floors and roof, had collapsed and let the columns down and, of course, that meant all the floors and interior walls as well.

"Architect Jones, a good and conscientious architect, had made those piers so excessively large the contractor thought it no sin to wheel barrows full of broken brick and stone into the hearts of them. They were found rotten at the core where the columns stood. Poor Architect Jones! He was now guilty of manslaughter—tried by a jury of his peers and condemned. He never built another building."

How often during our life he went back to that terrible memory which deeply affected his psyche at that time: "My life became restless, everything looked grim, my dissatisfaction was growing in the academic atmosphere which carried much too little inspiration for creative thinking and much too much of needless information. It was boring to me. Ideas were seething in me, disturbing me because of the lack of action."

He became increasingly restless and tried to find an outlet in devouring great books. Goethe, in particular, appealed to him at that time. He told me that in those early years he had seen a cast of Goethe's hands which were amazingly like his; and he was very pleased. But reading the great books did not release the mounting tension. He could bear no longer the force within him which was driving him to creative action. He confided his state to his mother and suggested that he go to Chicago to work for an architect, so that he could put his hand to real architectural work. He wanted to leave with her blessing. She wrote to his Uncle Jenkin Lloyd Jones, who was building a church there at the time. His reply was *no*; he believed strongly that Anna's son should remain in Madison to finish his education. Unfortunately, his mother agreed with her brother.

There was only one course for him to take. He pawned his favorite copy of Plutarch's *Lives*, a set of Gibbon's *Decline and Fall of the Roman Empire*, some other books from his father's library and a mink collar his mother had sewn on his overcoat, bought his ticket and with "seven dollars in his pocket" departed for his destiny.

THE BEGINNING OF WORK

He arrived by train at six o'clock in the evening. Years later he told me that the contrast between the quiet small town of Madison and the huge black-sooted city of Chicago was a severe shock to his senses, a chaos of noise and ugliness. But later on our frequent trips to Chicago he often said that it was a beautiful city with its glorious lake.

After the first shock he began to orient himself. Walking on Washington Street he saw a poster on the Chicago Opera House—the ballet was being performed that night—and he went in. "All of a sudden," he reminisced to me one day, "right in the middle of the show, the image of my mother rose between me and the stage, and a wave of regret and pain came over me. I felt the need to contact her immediately. I left the theater and all the way in the cable car which took me to my destination on Randolph Street I wrote her a long letter in my mind, begging her forgiveness. Then the tremendous impact of amassed impressions suddenly left me completely exhausted and when I reached the Brigg's house on Randolph Street, I fell asleep—dead to the world."

The next day he began his rounds of the architectural offices and after four days of searching he came to the office of J. L. Silsbee, where he met Cecil Corwin, a sympathetic, sensitive man, to whom he was instantly drawn. Corwin saw the drawings which the young architect had

CECIL CORWIN

made and recommended him highly to Silsbee. He got the job right away. In the evening he was invited to Corwin's house and from then on they became very close friends. Later that night he wrote his mother the letter he had had in his mind for several days. "I must say that I was greatly relieved in every way," he told me, "because I could also write to her that I had a job."

He found the work at Silsbee's easy, too easy perhaps. He became restless again and went to work for another firm, Beers, Clay and Dutton, but here he discovered that he was not ready for the complex work entrusted to him. He had to learn much more before he could design up to his own standard of what constituted good design. He returned to Mr. Silsbee who took him back gladly—at an increase in salary. While working in Silsbee's office he read in the papers about the great Auditorium which was just beginning to be built in Chicago. The work of its architects, Adler and Sullivan, rose like that of giants in the midst of Chicago's drab buildings, and he was electrified; he could not understand how he had not gone to their office in the first place.

It must have been providential that he should at that very time have been told by a young architect that there was an opening in the office of Adler and Sullivan! He felt badly about the prospect of leaving the office where he worked side by side with his friend Cecil Corwin, but Corwin himself encouraged him to go, assuring him that he had already learned all he could in Silsbee's firm.

He went at once to see Louis Sullivan, who asked him to make some drawings and come back with them. Two days later he returned to the

LOUIS H. SULLIVAN

DANKMAR ADLER

Adler and Sullivan office. Mr. Sullivan looked at his drawings and the following Monday morning Frank Lloyd Wright went to work—to spend seven years with his master. He later wrote: "That was how I got into the Adler and Sullivan office and how I first met the master for whose influence, affection and comradeship I have never ceased to feel gratitude."

The rest is history. The young man became "a good pencil in the Master's hand," and his reverence for Lieber Meister, as he always called him, turned into a lifetime friendship. Besides architecture they had much they shared together to weld their relationship: music, literature, philosophy, sculpture. The young architect's admiration for both Louis Sullivan and Dankmar Adler, "the big chief," grew stronger with each year of their life and work together. The relationship resulted in the most productive years in the history of architecture.

DRAWING SHOWN BY F.LL.W. IN 1888 TO LOUIS H. SULLIVAN.

Forty years later my husband showed me a drawing which he had inscribed: "Drawing shown to Lieber Meister when applying for a job." Done in 1888 when he was nineteen years old, it is an exquisite poem. Its lines are so delicate, so tender that it looks as though the sheer transparent spirit of a building had settled lightly on the paper. One's breath is held lest it vanish. Such was the power of Frank Lloyd Wright's genius.

Louis Sullivan made it possible for him to build his own house in Oak Park by advancing the money for the project to his apprentice who paid it back out of his wages for five years. In the meantime he accepted a commission for a house which he designed nights in his own studio.

It was through such a heedless young impulse on his part that a misunderstanding arose between him and Louis Sullivan, which became an issue neither of them could dissolve. Frank Lloyd Wright was in serious trouble. He appealed to Mr. Adler. "The big chief" interceded in his behalf with Louis Sullivan who, even more offended by this, imperiously declared to the young architect that his act was unforgivable. Harsh words were said. The young man of course felt that he was in the wrong, but he could not control the force which was driving him now on another course—his own work in architecture.

It was twelve years before he met his Lieber Meister again. Their friendship was too profound to have been fundamentally affected, and they remained close until Louis Sullivan's death.

To fit himself into a society which lived by long-established rules and standards often seemed impossible, but to Frank Lloyd Wright suffering only presented an incentive to action. He rebelled against outlived forms; it was impossible to build anything new on top of something that was already crumbling. He was already beginning to foresee a new society based upon a principle of architectural beauty, which could change not only the physical aspect but the social structure of the world. In 1957, nearly seventy years later, he said to the Taliesin Fellowship in Arizona:

"I think you can forgive a man his destructive propensities if he has a better idea to propose and is destructive only in order that he can plant it where something that may be worthless is growing. You cannot do much with a spirit that is preoccupied with worthless matters. To destroy such a condition in society may cause great suffering for the time being, but it is beneficent suffering and I think suffering is absolutely essential to growth. Whatever we see in nature has suffered in order that it might grow. In the process of its development it has suffered all kinds of hardship, without which there could be no growth.

"Louis Sullivan used to say he hated the wind, it was the enemy of all growing things. But I think he was wrong. Watch the movements of the trees, the plants and the cactus when the wind blows strongly, and you can see them exercising; you can see how fiber is developed in them and made necessary to their lives and how the very shape of the leaves, the very pattern, has been modified by the wind. Without that experience it would be weak and inconsequential, relatively speaking. While the wind is the adverse element, where growth is concerned, it is also the great developer. You can put adversity experienced by a human being into that category. However, I would not suggest that you look for trouble, because you will find enough of it anyway, just as the plant finds enough wind, through adversity, to become what it is.

"Look at that palm there, an amazing development, quite unexpected; if you study its structure you will see how it was designed to overcome the wind, the conflicting currents of air that toss it around and would tear it down but for something mysteriously planted in it that gave it the pattern of strength to be what it is.

"Of course, that is what we call God. That is all we know of Him. That is as far as we are going to get with any study we have to make of the great idea behind it all. And we call it God. It is all part of architecture, man's building is subject to all those inimical influences, along with the law of gravity, the violence of the wind, the pouring of the elements, the rain, and it has to be constructed to stand there like that plant, with an original idea in it and its construction, suited to its continuing life, according to the nature of its being. A building is a plant, subject to the same laws on high, and deep within, that the plant is subject to, and so, the study of Nature is the only study for an architect or an artist or anybody that wants to create anything."

(ABOVE) DETAIL OF PALM AT FAR LEFT, TALIESIN WEST, NEAR SCOTTSDALE, ARIZONA.

THE NEW SIMPLICITY

It was 1893—after the period with Adler and Sullivan had come to a close—and Frank Lloyd Wright now had his first job on his own, the Winslow House in River Forest, Illinois. "It burst on the view of that provincial suburb like the Prima Vera in full bloom," he wrote. "It was

WINSLOW HOUSE, RIVER FOREST, ILLINOIS

a new world to Oak Park and River Forest. That house became an attraction far and near. Incessantly it was courted and admired. Ridiculed, too, of course. Ridicule is always modeled on the opposite side of that shield. This first house soon began to sift the sheep from the goats . . ."

He established his own office in Chicago, in the Schiller Building which Louis Sullivan had designed, and clients who had seen the beauty and simplicity of the Winslow House began to gravitate toward him. Those early commissions are now landmarks in the development of a true American architecture: the Francis Apartments, the Husser and Heller homes, Lexington Terrace, the Wolff Lake Resort, and others.

In 1887, as a boy of eighteen, he had designed buildings for the Hillside Home School founded by his Aunts Nell and Jane. In 1896, his ideas were put to a critical test in the form of a windmill needed for

"ROMEO AND JULIET"—WINDMILL FOR MISSES LLOYD JONES, HILLSIDE, SPRING GREEN, WISCONSIN. SECTION BELOW

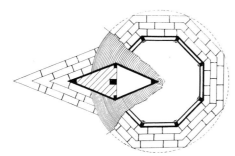

a new water system to be used for the school. He designed it as a tower with two interlocking forms, one a storm prow he named Romeo, "to do the work," and the other an octagonal form he called Juliet, "cuddled alongside to support and exalt him." The builder to whom the plans were submitted laughed; the idea was crazy; this tower would fall at the first beat of the wind. But his aunts had faith in the concept of their nephew who had written them that the tower would stand for twenty-five years. "I am afraid all of my uncles themselves may be gone before Romeo and Juliet."

The tower was built. That was more than seventy years ago. Romeo and Juliet still stand on the hill, though the Master-builder himself has left this world.

Frank Lloyd Wright's ideas of an organic architecture sprang freely from his creative mind, endless in variety, radiating from him as rays radiate from the sun, and in the course of his lifetime, they changed the architecture of the world.

"As I had gone to and fro between Oak Park and my work with Adler and Sullivan in Chicago," he wrote, "here at hand was the typical American dwelling of the 'monogoria' of earlier days, standing about on the Chicago prairie. That dwelling got there somehow to become typical. But by any faith in nature, implicit or explicit, it did not belong there. I had seen that in the light of the conception of architecture as natural. And ideas had naturally begun to come as to a more natural house. Each house I built, I longed for the chance to build another, and I soon got the chance. I was not the only one sick of hypocrisy and hungry for reality around there, I found.

"What was the matter with the kind of house I found on the prairie? Well, now that the 'monogoria' of my inexperience has become the clearer vision of experience—let me tell you in more detail.

"Just for a beginning let's say, that house *lied* about everything. It had no sense of Unity at all nor any such sense of Space as should belong to a free man among a free people in a free country. It was stuck up however it might be. It was stuck on whatever it happened to be. To take any one of those so-called 'homes' away would have improved the landscape and cleared the atmosphere. It was a box, too, that had to be cut full of holes to let in light and air and an especially ugly one to get in and out of, or else it was a clumsy 'gabled' chunk of roofed masonry similarly treated. Otherwise, 'joinery' reigned supreme. You know,—'Carpenter and Joiner' it used to read on the old signs. The floors were the only part of the house left plain and the housewife then covered those with a tangled rug-collection, because otherwise the floors were 'bare'—bare, only because one could not very well walk on jigsawing or turned spindles or plaster-ornament.

"It is not too much to say that as an architect my lot in Oak Park was cast with an inebriate lot of sinners hardened by habit against every human significance except one—why mention 'the one touch of nature that makes the whole world kin?' And I will venture to say that the aggregation was the worst the world ever saw—at the lowest aesthetic level in all history. Steam heat, plumbing and electric light were its only redeeming features.

"The first feeling therefore had been for a new simplicity. A new sense of simplicity as 'organic' had barely begun to take shape in my mind when the Winslow house was planned. But now it began in practice. Organic simplicity might be seen producing significant character in the harmonious order we call nature. All around was beauty in growing things. None were insignificant.

"I loved the prairie by instinct as a great simplicity—the trees, the flowers, the sky itself, thrilling by contrast.

"I saw that a little of height on the prairie was enough to look like much more—every detail as to height becoming intensely significant, breadths all falling short. Here was a tremendous spaciousness, but all sacrificed needlessly. All 'space' was cut up crosswise and cut up lengthwise into the fifty foot 'lot'—or would you have twenty-five feet less or twenty-five feet more? Salesmanship cut and parceled it out and sold it with no restrictions. In a great, new, free country there was then, everywhere, a characteristic tendency to 'huddle' and in consequence a mean tendency to tip everything in the way of human habitation up edgewise, instead of letting it lie comfortably and naturally flatwise with the ground. Nor has this changed, much, since automobilization made it stupid as an economic measure and criminal as a social habit. I had an idea that the horizontal planes in buildings, those planes parallel to earth, identify themselves with the ground—make the building belong to the ground. I began putting this idea to work.

"The buildings standing around there on the Chicago prairies were all tall and all tight. Chimneys were lean and taller still—sooty fingers threatening the sky. And besides them, sticking up almost as high, were the dormers.

"Dormers were elaborate devices—cunning little buildings complete in themselves—stuck on to the main roof-slopes to let 'help' poke heads out of the attic for air.

"Invariably the damp, sticky clay of the prairie was dug out for a basement under the whole house, and the rubble stone-walls of this dank basement always stuck above the ground a foot or several—and blinked, with half-windows.

"So the universal 'cellar' showed itself above ground as a bank of some kind of masonry running around the whole house, for the house to sit up on—like a chair. The lean upper house-walls of the usual two floors above this stone or brick basement were wood and set up on top of this masonry chair. The wood walls were clapboarded and painted, or else shingled and stained. Preferably house walls were both sided and shingled and mixed, up and down, together or with moldings crosswise. These over-dressed wood house walls had cut in them or cut out of them, to be precise, big holes for the big cat and little holes for the little cat to get in or get out. Or for ulterior purposes of light and air. These house walls were be-corniced or bracketed up at the top into the tall, purposely, profusely complicated roof, dormers plus. The whole roof as well as the roof as a whole was ridged and tipped, swanked and gabled to madness before they would allow it to be either watershed or shelter. The whole exterior was bedeviled, that is to say, mixed to puzzle-pieces, with corner-boards, panel-boards, window-frames, corner-blocks, plinth-blocks, rosettes, fantails, ingenious and jigger work in general. This was the only way 'they' seemed to have, then, of 'putting on the style.' The scrollsaw and turning lathe were at that moment the honest means to this fashionable mongering by the wood-butcher and to this entirely moral end.

"Unless the householder of the period were poor indeed, usually the ingenious corner tower as seen in the monogoria eventuated into a candle-snuffer dome, a spire, an inverted rutabaga or radish or onion —or what is your favorite vegetable? Always elaborate bay-windows and fancy porches rallied 'ring a round a rosie'—this imaginative corner fetich. And all this fetich the builders of the period could do, nearly as well, in brick or stone.

"It was an impartial society. All materials looked pretty much alike to it in that day.

"Simplicity was as far from all this scrap-pile as the pandemonium of the barnyard is far from music. But it was all easy enough for the architect. All he had to do was to call, 'Boy, take down No. 37, and put a bay-window on it for the lady.'

"The first thing to do in building the new house was to get rid of the attic and therefore of the dormer, get rid of the useless 'heights' below it. Next, get rid of the unwholesome basement, entirely, yes absolutely—in any house built on the prairie. Instead of lean, brick chimneys, bristling up everywhere to hint at 'Judgment' from steep roofs, I could see necessity for one chimney only. A broad generous one, or at most, two, these kept low-down on gently sloping roofs or perhaps flat roofs. The big fireplace in the house below became now a place for a real fire, and justified the great size of this chimney outside. A real fireplace at that time was extraordinary. There were mantels instead. A 'mantel' was a marble frame for a few coals. Or it was a piece of wooden furniture with tile stuck in it around a 'grate,' the whole set slam up against the wall. An insult to comfort. So the *integral* fireplace became an important part of the building itself in the houses I was allowed to build out there on the prairie.

"Comforting to see the fire burning deep in the masonry of the house itself.

"Taking a human being for my 'scale' I brought the whole house down in height to fit a normal one—ergo, 5′ 8″ tall, say. Believing in no other scale than the human being I broadened the mass out all I possibly could, brought it down into spaciousness. It has been said that were I three inches taller (I am 5′8½″ tall) all my houses would have been quite different in proportion. Perhaps.

"House walls were now to be started at the ground on a cement or stone water-table that looked like a low platform under the building, and usually was. But the house walls were stopped at the second story window sill level, to let the bedrooms come through above in a continuous window-series under the broad eaves of a gently sloping, overhanging roof. For in this new house the wall as an impediment to outside light and air and beauty was beginning to go. The old wall had been a part of the box in which only a limited number of holes were to be punched. It was still this conception of a wall which was with me when I designed the Winslow house. But after that my conception began to change.

"My sense of wall was not a side of a box. It was enclosure to afford protection against storm or heat when this was needed. But it was also increasingly to bring the outside world into the house, and let the inside of the house go outside. In this sense I was working toward the elimination of the wall as a wall to reach the function of a screen, as a means of opening up space, which, as control of building-materials improved, would finally permit the free use of the whole space without affecting the soundness of structure.

"The climate being what it was, violent in extremes of heat and cold, damp and dry, dark and bright, I gave broad protecting roof-shelter to the whole, getting back to the original purpose for which the cornice was designed. The underside of the roof-projections was flat and light in color to create a glow of reflected light that made upper rooms not dark, but delightful. The overhangs had double value: shelter and preservation for the walls of the house as well as diffusion of reflected light for the upper story, through the 'light screens' that took the place of the walls and were the windows.

GALE HOUSE, OAK PARK, ILLINOIS

"And at this time I saw a house primarily as livable interior space under ample shelter. I liked the sense of 'shelter' in the look of the building. I still like it.

"Then I went after the popular abuses. Eliminated odds and ends in favor of one material and a single surface as a flat plane from grade to eaves. I treated these flat planes usually as simple enclosing screens or else I again made a plain band around the second story above the window sills turned up over onto the ceiling beneath the eaves. This screen band would be of the same material as the underside of the eaves themselves, or what architects call the 'soffit.'

"The planes of the building parallel to the ground were all stressed —I liked to 'stress' them—to grip the whole to Earth. This parallel plane I called, from the beginning,—the plane of the third dimension. The term came naturally enough: really a spiritual interpretation of that dimension.

"Sometimes I was able to make the enclosing wall screen below this upper band of the second story—from the second story window sill clear down to the ground, a heavy 'wainscot' of fine masonry material resting on the cement or stone 'platform' laid on the foundation. I liked the luxury of masonry material, when my clients felt they could afford it.

"As a matter of form, too, I liked to see the projecting base or water-table of masonry set out over the foundation walls themselves, as a substantial 'visible' preparation for the building. I managed this by setting the studs of the walls to the inside of the foundation walls, instead of to the outside.

"All door and window tops were now brought into line with each other with only comfortable head clearage for the average human being.

"Eliminating the sufferers from the 'attic' enabled the roof to lie low.

"The house began to associate with the ground and become natural to its prairie site.

"And would the young man in Architecture believe that this was all 'new' then? Yes—not only new, but it was all destructive heresy—or ridiculous eccentricity. Stranger still all somewhat so today. But then it was all so *new* that what prospect I had of ever earning a livelihood by making houses was nearly wrecked. At first, 'they' called the houses 'dress reform' houses, because Society was just excited about that particular 'reform.' This simplification looked like some kind of 'reform' to the provincials.

"Oh, they called the new houses all sort of names that can not be repeated, but 'they' never found a better term for the work unless it was 'horizontal Gothic,' 'temperance Architecture' (with a sneer), etc. etc. I don't know how I escaped the accusation of another 'Renaissance-Japanese' or 'Bhutanese' from my complimentary academic contemporaries. Eclectics can imagine only eclecticism.

"What I have just described was all on the *outside* of the house. But it was there, chiefly, because of what had happened *inside*.

"Dwellings of that period were cut up, advisedly and completely, with the grim determination that should go with any 'cutting' process. The 'interiors' consisted of boxes beside boxes or inside boxes, called *rooms*. All boxes were inside a complicated outside boxing. Each domestic 'function' was properly box to box.

"I could see little sense in this inhibition, this cellular sequestration that implied ancestors familiar with penal institutions, except for the privacy of bedrooms on the upper floor. They were perhaps all right as 'sleeping boxes.'

"So I declared the whole lower floor as one room, cutting off the kitchen but semi-detached, on the ground floor. Then I screened various portions of the big room for certain domestic purposes, like dining or reading—receiving callers.

"There were no plans in existence like these at the time, but my clients were pushed toward these ideas as helpful to a solution of the vexed servant problem. Scores of unnecessary doors disappeared and no end of partition. Both clients and servants liked the new freedom. The house became more free as 'space' and more livable too. Interior spaciousness began to dawn.

"Thus an end to the cluttered house. Fewer doors; fewer window holes, though much greater window area; windows and doors lowered to convenient human heights. These changes made, the ceilings of the rooms could be brought down over on to the walls, by way of the horizontal broad bands of plaster on the walls themselves above the windows, colored the same as the room-ceilings. This would bring the ceiling-surface and color down to the very window tops. The ceilings

PLATE 82. AVERY COONLEY HOUSE, RIVERSIDE, ILLINOIS. INTERIOR VIEW

LIVING ROOM, COONLEY HOUSE, RIVERSIDE, ILLINOIS

thus expanded by way of the wall band above the windows gave generous overhead to even the small rooms.

"The sense of the whole was broadened, made plastic, too, by this means.

"Here entered the important new element of plasticity—as I saw it. And I saw it as indispensable element to the successful use of the machine. The windows would sometimes be wrapped around the building corners as emphasis of plasticity and sense of interior space. I fought for outswinging windows because the casement window associated the house with the out-of-doors, gave free openings, outward. In other words the so-called 'casement' was simple, more human in use and effect, so more natural. If it had not existed I should have invented it. But it was not used at that time in the United States so I lost many clients because I insisted upon it. The client usually wanted the 'guillotine' or 'double hung' window in use then. The guillotine was neither simple nor human. It was only expedient. I used it once in the Winslow house and rejected it thereafter forever. Nor at that time did

I entirely eliminate the wooden trim. I did make it 'plastic', that is to say, light and continuously flowing instead of the prevailing heavy 'cut and butt' carpenter work. No longer did 'trim,' so-called, look like 'carpenter work.' The machine could do it all perfectly well as I laid it out, in the search for 'quiet.' This plastic trim, too, enabled poor workmanship to be concealed. There was need of that trim to conceal much in the way of craftsmanship because machines versus the Union had already demoralized the workmen.

"The machine-resources of the period were so little understood that extensive drawings had to be made merely to show the mill-man what to leave off. But finally the trim thus became only a single, flat, narrow horizontal band running around the room walls at the top of the windows and doors and another one at the floors. Both were connected with narrow vertical thin wood bands that were used to divide the wall-surfaces of the whole room smoothly and flatly into color planes folded about the corners—exterior corners or interior corners—and the trim merely completed the window and door openings in this same plastic sense. When the handling of the interior had thus become wholly plastic instead of structural—a new element, as I have already said, had entered the prairie house architecture. Strangely enough an element that had not existed in architecture before, if architectural

VIEW INTO LIVING ROOM, ROBIE HOUSE, CHICAGO, ILLINOIS

history is to be credited. Not alone in the trim but in numerous ways too tedious to describe in words, this revolutionary sense of the *plastic* whole, began to work more and more intelligently and have fascinating unforeseen consequences. Here was something that began to organize itself. When several houses had been finished, compared with the house of the period there was very little of that house left standing. But that little was left standing up very high indeed. Nearly everyone had endured the house of the period as long as possible, judging by the appreciation of the change. Now all this probably tedious description is intended to indicate in bare outline how thus early there was an Ideal of organic Simplicity put to work, with historical consequences, in this country.

"Let me now put all this in clear outline for you. The main motives and inclinations were—and I enjoyed them all . . . and still enjoy them—

"First . . . to reduce the number of necessary parts of the house or the separate rooms to a minimum, and make all come together as free space—so subdivided that light, air and vista permeated the whole with a sense of unity.

"Second . . . to associate the building as whole with its site by extension and emphasis of the planes parallel to the ground, but keeping the floors off from the best part of the site, thus leaving that better part for use in connection with the use of the house. Extended level planes or long narrow levels were found useful in this connection.

"Third . . . to eliminate the rooms as boxes and the house itself as another boxing of the boxes, making all walls enclosing screens; ceilings and floors to flow the enclosing screens as one large enclosure of space, with minor or subordinate subdivisions only. And also to make all proportions more liberally human, eliminate waste space in structure and make structure more appropriate to material. The whole made more sensible and livable. Liberal is the best word. Extended straight lines or stream lines were useful in this.

"Fourth . . . to get the unwholesome basement up out of the ground, entirely above it, as a low pedestal for the living portion of the home, making the foundation itself visible as a low masonry platform on the ground on which the building would stand.

"Fifth . . . to harmonize all necessary openings to outside or inside with good human proportions and make them occur naturally, singly or in series, in the scheme of the whole building. Usually they now appeared as light screens—usually turning the corners—instead of walls, because chiefly the architecture of the house was expressed in the way these openings happened to such walls as were grouped about the rooms, anyway. The room was now the essential architectural expression. And there were to be no holes cut in walls anywhere or anyhow as holes are cut in a box, because this was not in keeping with the ideal of 'plastic'. Cutting holes was violence.

"I saw that the insensate, characterless flat surface, cut sheer, had geometric possibilities . . . but it has, also, the limitations of bare geometry. Such negation in itself is sometimes restful and continually useful—as a foil—but not as the side of a box.

"Sixth . . . to eliminate combinations of different materials in favor of mono-material so far as possible, and to use no ornament that did not come out of the nature of materials or construction to make the whole building clearer and more expressive as a place to live in and give the conception of the building appropriate revealing emphasis. Geometrical or straight lines were natural to the machinery at work in the building trades then, so the interiors took on this rectilinear character naturally.

"Seventh . . . to so incorporate all heating, lighting, plumbing that these mechanical systems became constituent parts of the building itself. These service features became architectural features. In this attempt the ideal of an organic architecture was at work.

"Eighth . . . to incorporate as organic architecture, so far as possible, furnishings, making them all one with the building, designing the equipment in simple terms for machine-work. Again, straight lines and rectilinear forms. Geometrical.

"Ninth . . . eliminate the decorator. He was all 'applique' and all efflorescence, if not all 'period'. Inorganic."

A NOBLE ROOM

The first emphatic protest against the tide of meaningless elaboration sweeping the United States . . . a simple cliff of brick and stone that had profound influence upon European architecture . . ." Frank Lloyd Wright said of the Larkin Building which he built in 1904 in Buffalo, New York. This great sealed block was full of new ideas which have since become part of the fabric of industrial buildings: fireproof, with furniture made of steel built into place, automatic chair-desks, wall water closets, hanging partitions, all to facilitate cleaning and ease the work process—practicality in stately beauty.

And shortly after that, in 1906, came Unity Temple, to which architects and students from every corner of the earth have come ever since in a constant stream to study its structure.

"Let us take Unity Temple to pieces in the thought of its architect," he wrote, " and see how it came to be the Unity Temple you now see—the prophet of Space."

"Had Doctor Johonnot, the Universalist pastor of Unity Church, been Fra Junipero the 'style' of Unity Temple would have been predetermined. Had he been Father Latour, it would have been Midi-Romanesque. Yes, and perhaps being what he was, he was entitled to

LARKIN BUILDING, BUFFALO, NEW YORK

the only tradition he knew—that of the little white New England Church, lean spire pointing to heaven—back East. If sentimentality were sense this might be so.

"But the pastor was out of luck. Circumstances brought him to yield himself up 'in the cause of architecture.' The straight line and the flat plane were to emerge as the cantilever slab.

"And to that cause everyone who undertakes to read what follows is called upon to yield. It should only be read after studying the plans and perspective of Unity Temple. Constant reference to the plan will be necessary if the matter is to come clear.

"Our building committee were all 'good men and true.' One of them, Charles E. Roberts, a mechanical engineer and inventor, enlightened in creation.

LARKIN BUILDING INTERIOR

BUILT-IN STEEL FURNITURE USED IN LARKIN BUILDING

"One, enlightened, is leaven enough in any Usonian lump. The struggle—it is always a struggle in architecture for the architect where 'good men and true' are concerned—began.

"First came the philosophy of the building.

"Human sensibilities are the strings of the instrument upon which the true artist plays his . . . 'abstract' . . . ? But why not avoid the symbol, as such? The symbol is too literal. It is become a form of Literature in the Art of Architecture.

"Let us abolish, in the art and craft of architecture, *literature* in any 'symbolic' form whatsoever. The sense of inner rhythm, deep planted in human sensibility, lives far above other considerations in Art.

"Then why the steeple of the little white church? Why *point* to heaven?

"I told the committee a story. Did they not know the tale of the holy man who, yearning to see God, climbed up and up the highest mountain—up and up on and to and up the highest relic of a tree there was on the mountain too? Ragged and worn, there he lifted up his eager perspiring face to heaven and called on 'God.' A voice . . . bidding him get down . . . go back!

"Would he really see God's face? Then he should go back, go down there in the valley below where his own people were—there only could *he* look upon God's countenance.

"Was not that 'finger' (the church steeple) pointing on high like the man who climbed on high to see HIM? A misleading symbol perhaps: a perversion of sentiment—that is to say, *sentimentality*.

"Was not the time come now to be more simple, to have more faith in man on his own Earth and less anxiety concerning his Heaven about which he could *know* nothing? Concerning this heaven he had never received any testimony from his own senses.

"Why not, then, build a temple, not to God in that way—(more sentimental than sense)—but build a temple to man, appropriate to his uses as a meeting place, in which to study man himself for his God's sake? A modern meeting-house and good-time place.

"Build a beautiful ROOM proportioned to this purpose. Make it beautiful in this *simple* sense. A *natural* building for natural Man.

"The pastor was a 'liberal.' His liberality was thus challenged, his reason piqued and the curiosity of all aroused.

"What would such a building be like. They said they could imagine no such thing.

"'That's what you came to me for,' I ventured. 'I can imagine it and will help you create it.'

"Promising the building committee something tangible to look at soon—I sent them away, they not knowing, quite, whether they were foolish, fooled, or fooling with a fool.

"That ROOM; it began to be that same night.

"Enter now the realm of architectural ideas . . .

"The first idea was to keep a noble ROOM in mind, and let the room shape the whole edifice, *let the room inside be the architecture outside.*

"What shape? Well, the answer lay, in what material? There was only one material to choose as the church funds were $45,000, to 'church' 400 people in 1906. Concrete was still cheap.

"Concrete alone could do it. But even concrete as it was in use at that time meant wood 'forms' and some other material than concrete for outside facing. They were in the habit of covering the concrete with brick or stone, plastering and furring the inside of the walls. Plastering the outside would be cheaper than brick or stone but wouldn't stick to concrete in our climate. Why not make the wooden boxes or forms so

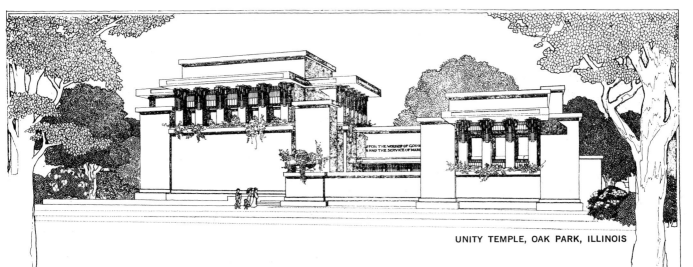

the concrete could be cast in them as separate blocks and masses, these separate blocks and masses grouped about an interior space in some such way as to preserve this desired sense of the interior space in the appearance of the whole building? And the block-masses be left as themselves with no 'facing.' That would be cheap and permanent and true.

"Then, how to cover the separate features and concrete masses as well as the sacrosanct space from the extremes of northern weather. What roof?

"What had concrete to offer as a cover shelter? The slab—of course. The reinforced slab. Nothing else if the building was to be thorough-bred, meaning built in character out of one material.

"Too monumental, all this? Too forthright for my committee, I feared. Would a statement so positive as that final slab over the whole seem irreligious to them? Profane in their eyes? Why?

"The flat slab was direct. It would be 'nobly' simple. The wooden forms or molds in which concrete buildings must at that time be cast were always the chief item of expense, so to repeat the use of a single one as often as possible was desirable, even necessary. Therefore a building all four sides alike looked like the thing. This, in simplest terms, meant a building square in plan. That would make their temple a cube. A noble form.

"The slab, too, belonged to the cube by nature. 'Credo simplicitas.'

"That form is most imaginative and 'happy' that is most radiant with the 'aura' or overtone of superform.

"Geometric shapes through human sensibility have thus acquired to some extent human significance as, say, the cube or square, integrity; the circle or sphere, infinity; the straight line, rectitude; if long drawn out . . . repose; the triangle . . . aspiration, etc.

"There was no money to spend in working on the concrete mass outside or with it after it was once cast.

"Good reason, this, if no other, for getting away from any false facing. Couldn't the surface be qualified in the casting process itself so this whole matter of veneered 'Facade' could be omitted with good effect? This was later the cause of much experiment, with what success may be seen.

"Then the Temple itself—as yet in my mind—began to take shape. The site was noisy. By the Lake Street car-tracks. Therefore it seemed best to keep the building closed on the three front sides and enter it from a court at the center of the lot.

"So Unity Temple itself, with the thoughts in mind I have just expressed, arrived easily enough, but there was a secular side to Universalist church activities—entertainment—Sunday school, feasts, etc.

"To embody these latter with the temple would spoil the simplicity of the room—the noble ROOM—in the service of MAN for the worship of GOD.

"So finally I put this secular space as 'Unity House,' a long free room to the rear of the lot, as a separate building to be subdivided by moveable screens, on occasions. It thus became a separate building but harmonious with the Temple—the entrance to both to be the connecting link between them. (See the plan.) That was that.

"To go back to the Temple itself. What kind of 'square room'? How effect the form of cube and best serve the purpose of audience room?

"Should the pulpit be put toward the street and let the congregation come in and go out at the rear in the usual disrespectful church fashion so the pastor missed contact with his flock? And the noise of the street cars on Lake Street come in?

"No. Why not put the pulpit at the entrance side at the rear of the square Temple entirely cut off from the street and bring the congregation into the room at the sides and on a lower level so those entering would be imperceptible to the audience? This would make the incomers as little a disturbance or challenge to curiosity as possible.

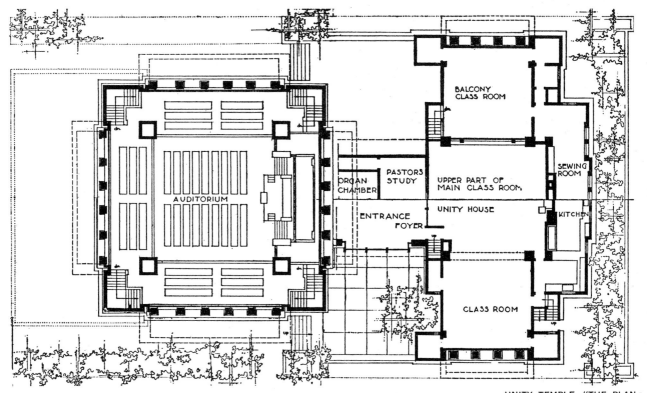

The following labels appear on the plan:

BALCONY CLASS ROOM

SEWING ROOM

PASTORS STUDY

ORGAN CHAMBER

UPPER PART OF MAIN CLASS ROOM

AUDITORIUM

UNITY HOUSE

KITCHEN

ENTRANCE FOYER

CLASS ROOM

UNITY TEMPLE. "THE PLAN FIRST BEGAN THE DESTRUCTION OF THE BOX, AND THE EMPHASIS OF INTERIOR SPACE AS THE REALITY OF THE BUILDING SUBSEQUENTLY CARRIED ON." — F.LL.W.

This would preserve the quiet and the dignity of the room itself. Out of that thought came the depressed foyer or 'cloister' corridor either side leading from the main entrance lobby at the center to the stairs in the near and far corners of the room. Those entering the room in this way could see into the big room but not be seen by those already seated within it.

"And when the congregation rose to disperse here was opportunity to move forward toward their pastor and by swinging wide doors open beside the pulpit let the flock pass forward and out by the minister and find themselves directly in the entrance loggia from which they had first come in. They had entered the big room by the depressed entrances at the sides from this same entrance to enter the big room. It seemed more respectful, too, to let them go out thus toward the pulpit than to turn their backs upon their minister to go out as is usual in most churches. This scheme gave the minister's flock to him to greet. Few could escape. The position of the pulpit in relation to the entrance made this reverse movement possible.

"So this was done.

"The room itself—size determined by comfortable seats with leg-room for four hundred people—was built with four interior free standing posts to carry the overhead structure. These concrete posts were hollow and became free-standing ducts to insure economic and uniform distribution of heat. The large supporting posts were so set in plan as to form a double tier of alcoves on four sides of this room. Flood these side-alcoves with daylight from above: get a happy sense of a happy cloudless day into the room. And with this feeling for light the center ceiling between the four great posts became a skylight, daylight sifting through between the intersections of big concrete beams, filtering through amber glass ceiling lights. Thus the interior light would, rain or shine, have the warmth of sunlight. Artificial lighting could take place there at night as well. This scheme of lighting was integral, gave diffusion and kept the room space clear.

"The spacious wardrobes between the depressed foyers either side of the room and under the auditorium itself, were intended to give opportunity to the worshippers to leave their wraps before entering the worshipful room. And this wardrobe would work as well for the entertainments in the long room to the rear because it was just off the main entrance lobby.

"The secular hall—Unity House—itself, was tall enough to have galleries at each side of the central space—convertible into class-room space.

"A long kitchen connected to each end of the secular space was added to the rear of Unity House for the Temple 'feasts.'

"The pastor's offices and study came of themselves over the entrance lobby the connection between the two buildings. The study thus looked down through swinging windows into the secular hall—while it was just a convenient step behind the pulpit.

"All this seemed in proper order. Seemed natural enough.

"Now for proportion—for the 'concrete' expression of concrete itself in this natural arrangement—the ideal of an organic whole by now well in mind.

"For observe, what has actually taken place so far is only reasoned arrangement. The 'plan' with an eye to an exterior in the realm of ideas but only 'felt' in imagination.

"First came the philosophy of the thing in the little story repeated to the trustees. All artistic creation has its own—the first condition of creation. However, some would smile and say, 'the result of it.'

"Second there was the general purpose of the whole to consider in each part: a matter of this reasoned arrangement. This arrangement must be made with a sense of the yet-unborn-whole in the mind, to be blocked out as appropriate to concrete masses cast in wooden boxes. Holding all this diversity together in a preconceived direction is really no light matter but it is the condition of creation. Imagination conceives here the PLAN suitable to the material and the purpose—seeing the probable—possible form of the eventual whole.

"Imagination reigns supreme, when now the *form* the whole will naturally take, must be seen.

"And we have arrived at the question of *style*.

"But if all this preliminary planning has been well conceived that question in the main is settled. The matter may be intensified, made eloquent or modified and quieted. It cannot much change. This matter of style is Organic by now. That is to say, the concrete forms of Unity Temple will take the character of all we have so far done, if all we have so far done is harmonious with the principle we are waking to work. The structure will now put forth its forms as the tree puts forth branches and foliage—if we do not stultify it, do not betray it in some way.

"We do not choose the style. Style is what this is now and what *we are*. A thrilling moment, this, in any architect's experience. He is about to see the countenance of something he is invoking. Out of this sense of order and his love of the beauty of life—something is to be born maybe to live long as a message of hope and joy or as a curse to his kind. *His* message he feels. None the less is it 'theirs'. Rather more. And it is out of love and understanding such as this on the part of the architect that a building is born to bless or curse those it is built to ennoble.

"Bless them if they will see and understand. Curse them and be cursed by them if either they or their architect should fail to under-stand. . . . This is the faith and the fear in the architect as he makes ready—to draw his design on paper.

"In all artists it is the same, I imagine.

"Now comes the time to brood—to suffer doubt and burn with eagerness. To test bearings—and prove assumed ground by putting all together to definite scale on paper. Preferably small scale at first. Then larger. Finally still larger scale studies of parts. They are never enough —and seem endless.

"This pure white sheet of paper! Ready now—at last for the graphic logic of the plan.

"T-square, triangle, scale—seductive invitation lying upon the spotless surface.

"Temptation!

" 'Boy! Go tell Black Kelly to make a blaze there in the work-room fireplace! Ask Brown-Sadie if it's too late to have baked Bermudas for supper! Then go ask your mother—I shall hear her in here—to play something—Bach preferred, or Beethoven if she prefers.'

"An aid to creative effort, the open fire. What a friend to the laboring artist, the poetic baked-onion. Real encouragement is great music.

"Yes, and what a poor creature, after all, creation comes singing through. About like catgut and horsehair in the hands of Sarasate.

"Night labor at the draughting board is best for intense creation. It may continue uninterrupted.

"Meantime 'reflections' are passing in the architect's mind—'architectural design is abstraction of nature-elements in purely geometric terms'—is that what we ought to call pure design? . . . But—nature-pattern and nature-texture in materials themselves often do approach conventionalization (or the abstract) to such a degree as to be superlative means all ready to the designer's hand to qualify, stimulate and enrich his own efforts. . . . What texture this concrete mass? Why not its own gravel? How to bring the gravel clean on the surface?

"Here was reality. Yes, the 'fine thing' is reality. Always reality?

"Realism, the subgeometric, is however the abuse of this fine thing.

"Keep the straight lines clean and significant, the flat planes expressive and clean cut. But let texture of material come into them. Quiet!

"Reality is spirit . . . Essence is brooding just behind aspect!

"Seize it, boy—after all, reality is supergeometric, casting a spell or a 'charm' over any geometry form, as such, in itself.

"Yes, so it seems to me, that this is what it means to be an artist . . . *to seize this essence* always brooding just behind *aspect*. These questionings arising each with its train of thought by the way, as he works.

"It is morning! To bed for a while!

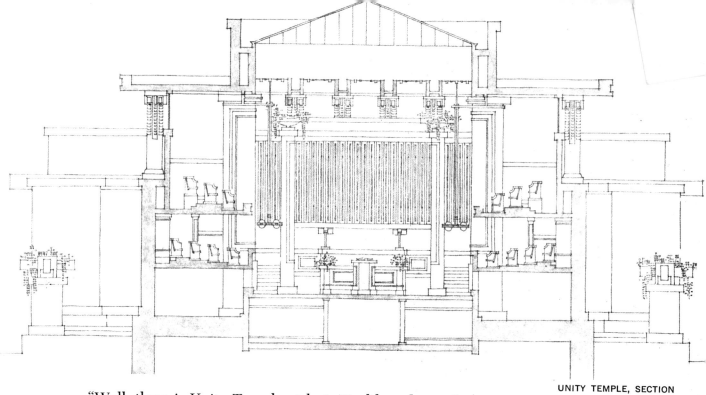

"Well, there is Unity Temple at last. Health and soundness in it, though still far to go.

"But here we have penciled on the sheet of paper, in the main, the plan, section and elevation as in the drawings illustrated here, all except the exterior of 'Unity House', as the room for secular recreation came to be called.

"To establish harmony between these two buildings of such widely separate function proved difficult, true—utterly exasperating.

"Another series of continuous concentrations—lasting hours at a time for several days. How to keep the noble scale of the temple in the design of this subordinate mass of the secular hall and yet not falsify the function of that noble mass? The ideal of an organic architecture is most severe discipline for the human imagination. I came to know that full well. And, always, some minor concordance like this takes more time, taxes concentration more than all besides. To vex the architect, this minor element now becomes a major problem. How many schemes I have thrown away because some one minor feature would not come true to form!

"Thirty-four studies were necessary to arrive at this concordance as it is now seen. Unfortunately they are lost with thousands of those of other buildings. The fruit of similar struggles to coordinate and perfect them as organic entities—I wish I had kept them all.

"Unity House looks easy enough now, for it is right enough as I see it.

"But this 'harmony of the whole' where diverse functions cause diverse masses to occur is no light affair for the architect—nor ever will be if he keeps his ideal high.

"Now observe the plans and elevations, then see the model or photograph of the building. See, now, how all that has taken place is showing itself *as it is* for what it is.

"A new industrial method for the use of a new material is invented and revealed. Roof slabs—attic walls—screen walls—posts and glass screens enclose, as architecture, a great room. In themselves they are little or nothing.

"The sense of the great room is not only preserved—*it may be seen as the soul of the design.* Instead of being built into the heart of a block of sculptured building material, out of sight, sacrosanct space is merely screened in . . . it comes through as the living 'motif' of the architecture.

"The grammar of such style as is seen here is simply and logically determined by the concrete mass and flat layer formation of the slab and wooden box construction of the square room, proportioned according to concrete-nature—or the nature of the concrete cast in boxes. All is assembled about coveted interior space, now visibly cherished by ceilings, walls and floors.

"Such architectural forms as there are, each to each as all in all, are cubical in form, to be cast solid in wooden boxes. But *one* motif only may be seen, *the 'inside' becoming 'outside.'* The groups of monoliths in their changing phases, square in character, do not depart from that single IDEA. Here we have something of the organic integrity in structure out of which issues character as an aura. The consequence is always-style. A stylish development of the square becoming the cube.

"Understanding Unity Temple one may respect it. It serves its purpose well. It was easy enough to build. Its harmonies are bold and striking, but genuine in melody. The 'square', too positive in statement for current 'taste', the straight line and the flat plane uncompromising? Yes. But here is entity again to prove that architecture may, if need be, live again as the nature-of-the-thing in terms of building material. Here is one building rooted in such modern conditions of work, materials and thought, as prevailed at the time when it was built. Singleminded in motif. Faithful in form to the concept.

"Out of this coordination will come many subsequent studies in refinement—correction of correlation, scale tests for integration. Overcoming difficulties in detail, in the effort to keep all clean and simple as a whole, is continued during the whole process of planning and building to the last moment.

"Many studies in detail yet remain to be made, perhaps, to determine what further may be left out to protect the design. These studies seem never to end, and in this sense, no organic building may ever be 'finished'. The complete goal of the ideal of organic architecture is never reached. Nor need be. What worthwhile ideal is ever reached?

"But we have enough now on paper to make a perspective drawing to go with the plan for the committee of 'good men and true' to see. Usually a committee has only the sketch to consider. But it is impossible to present a 'sketch' when working in this method. The building as a whole must be all in order before the 'sketch' not after it.

"Unity Temple is a complete building on paper, already. There is no 'sketch' and there never has been one."

UNITY TEMPLE, OAK PARK, ILLINOIS

CONQUEST OF THE EARTHQUAKE

The flow of great works continued, each building a battle carried to successful conclusion against rooted convention.

In 1908 there was the Coonley house; in 1909, the Robie house; in 1910, a trip to Europe to prepare the drawings for the great Wasmuth portfolio. In 1911 he built Taliesin I on the hill above his ancestral valley. There he prepared a number of new projects, including Midway Gardens, which frequently took him to Chicago to supervise the work.

ROBIE HOUSE, CHICAGO, ILLINOIS

COONLEY HOUSE, RIVERSIDE, ILLINOIS

MIDWAY GARDENS, CHICAGO, ILLINOIS

VIEW FROM TALIESIN, SPRING GREEN, WISCONSIN

Then in 1914, a tragic fire swept Taliesin off the hill, but being in love with his home-valley, he rebuilt the house as soon as time permitted and in 1915 Taliesin II stood in its place. That same year, he received the commission to build the Imperial Hotel in Tokyo, which took him across the Pacific to supervise its construction, and while in Japan, he designed a school and several residences.

In the early twenties he returned to the United States, taking up temporary residence in California, where he designed and built the Hollyhock House for Aline Barnsdall; the house known as *La Miniatura* for Mrs. Millard; the Storer, Freeman and Ennis houses—all built of concrete block with integral patterns, giving new distinction to what had been considered a commonplace material.

He made frequent trips to Tokyo to look after the building which was destined to become famous all over the world after it survived the earthquake in September 1923, remaining intact while buildings around it crumbled into heaps of rubble.

BARNSDALL ("HOLLYHOCK") HOUSE, OLIVE HILL, LOS ANGELES, CALIFORNIA. "CHARACTERISTIC CALIFORNIA ROMANZA, EMBODYING THE CHARACTERISTIC FEATURES OF THE REGION. . . ."—F.LL.W.

MILLARD HOUSE ("LA MINIATURA"), PASADENA, CALIFORNIA—"THE FIRST CONCRETE BLOCK HOUSE TO EMPLOY THE TEXTILE-BLOCK SYSTEM INVENTED BY MYSELF SEVERAL YEARS BEFORE."—F.LL.W.

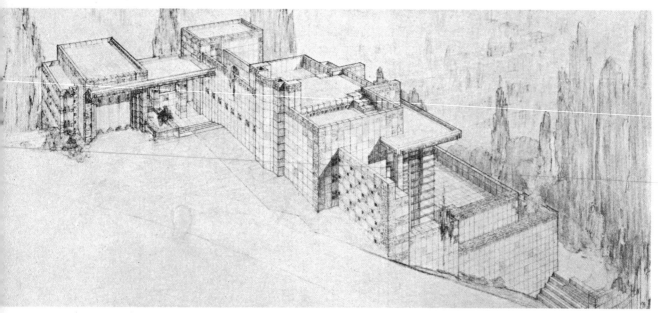

FREEMAN HOUSE, LOS ANGELES, CALIFORNIA

STORER HOUSE, LOS ANGELES, CALIFORNIA

(ABOVE AND BELOW) ENNIS HOUSE, LOS ANGELES, CALIFORNIA

"A social clearing house, call it a hotel, became necessary to official Japan as a consequence of new foreign interest in the Japanese," Frank Lloyd Wright writes. "A new hotel became necessary, because no foreigner, no matter how cultivated, could live on the floor as the Japanese do with any grace or comfort. It was also necessary for another reason: a Japanese gentleman does not entertain strangers, no matter how gentle, within his family circle. So the building would be more a place for entertainment, with private supper rooms, banquet hall, theatre and cabaret, than it would be a hotel.

"No foreign architect yet invited to work in Japan ever took off his hat to the Japanese and respected either Japanese conditions or traditions. And yet those aesthetic traditions are at the top among the noblest in the world. When I accepted the commission to design and build their building it was my instinct and definite intention not to insult them. Were they not a feature of my first condition, the ground? They were. The Japanese were more their own ground than any people I knew.

"So while making their building 'modern' in the best sense, I meant to leave it a sympathetic consort to Japanese buildings. I wanted to show the Japanese how their own conservation of space and the soul of their own religious shinto, which is 'be clean,' might, in the use of all materials, take place as effectively for them indoors in sound masonry construction when on their feet as it had taken place for them when they were down upon their knees in their own inspired carpentry.

"I meant to show them how to use our new civilizing-agents—call them plumbing, electrification, and heating—without such outrage to the art of building as we ourselves were practicing and they were then copying. I intended to make all these appurtenance systems a practical and aesthetic part of the building itself. It was to be given a new simplicity by making it a complete whole within itself.

"Mechanical systems should be an asset to life and so an asset to architecture. They should be no detriment to either. Why shouldn't the Japanese nation make the same coordination of furnishing and building when they came to be at home on their feet that they had so wonderfully made for themselves at home on their knees?

"And I believed I could show them how to build an earthquake-proof masonry building.

"In short, I desired to help Japan make the transition from wood to masonry, and from her knees to her feet, without too great loss of her own accomplishments in culture. And I wished to enable her to overcome some of the inherent weaknesses of her building system where the temblor was a constant threat to her happiness and to her very life.

"There was this natural enemy to all building whatsoever: the temblor. And, as I well knew, the seismograph in Japan is never still. The presence of the temblor, an affair of the ground, never left me while I planned and for four years or more worked upon the plans and structure of the new hotel. Earthquakes I found to be due to wave movement of the ground. Because of wave movement, foundations like long piles oscillate and rock the structure. Heavy masses of masonry inevitably would be wrecked. The heavier the masonry the greater the wreck.

"The feature of the ground that was the site itself was a flat 500-by-300-foot plot of ground composed of sixty feet of liquid mud overlaid by eight feet of filled soil. The filling was about the consistency of hard cheese. The perpetual water level stood within fifteen inches of the level of the ground. In short, the building was to stand up on an ancient marsh, an arm of the bay that had been filled in when Tokyo became the capital of the empire.

"But the mud beneath the filling seemed to me a good cushion to relieve earthquake shocks. A building might float upon the mud somewhat as a battleship floats on salt water. Float the building upon the mud? Why not? And since it must float, why not extreme lightness combined with the tenuity and flexibility that are a property of steel instead of the great weight necessary to the usually excessive rigidity which, no matter how rigid, could never be rigid enough. Probably the answer was a building made flexible as the two hands thrust together, fingers interlocked, yielding to movement yet resilient to return to position when force exerted upon its members and membranes ceased. Why fight the force of the quake on its own terms? Why not go with it and come back unharmed? Outwit the quake?

"That was how the nature of the site, the ground, entered into the conception of the building. Now, to carry out in detail these initial perceptions.

"I took a preliminary year in which to acquire necessary data, making tests for the new type of foundation. Finally flexible foundations, economical too, were provided by driving tapered wooden piles, only eight feet long, into the strata of filled soil, pulling them out and throwing in concrete immediately, to form the thousands of small piers or concrete pins two feet apart on centers upon which the jointed footing courses were laid. Nine pile drivers dotted the ground, each with its band of singing women pulling on the ropes, one for each pair of hands.

"The good sense of careful calculation so far: now what about the superstructure?

"The building was going native, so intensive hand methods would have to be used and native materials too. The nature of the design therefore should be something hand methods could do better than machinery. It was impossible to say how far we could go in any direction with machines, probably not very far.

"Evidently the straight line and flat plane to which I had already been committed by machines in America should be modified in point of style if I would respect the traditions of the people to whom the building would belong. The Japanese, centuries ago, had come nearer the ideal of an organic architecture in their dwellings than any civilized race on earth. The ideals we have been calling organic are even now best exemplified in their wood and paper dwellings where they lived on their knees. As I have already said, I wanted to help the Japanese get to their feet indoors and learn to live in fireproof masonry buildings, without loss of their native aesthetic prestige where the art of architecture was a factor. Trained by the disasters of centuries to build lightly on the ground, the wood and paper homes natural to them are kindled by any spark. When fire starts it seldom stops short of several hundred homes, sometimes destroys thousands, and ends in complete destruction of a city. After the irresistible wave movements have gone shuddering and jolting through the earth, changing all overnight in immense areas, islands disappearing, new ones appearing, mountains laid low and valleys lifted up taking awful toll of human life, then come the flames! Conflagration always at the end.

"The cost of metal frames and sash at that time was prohibitive, but the plans were made for an otherwise completely fireproof building and the designs were so made that all architectural features were practical necessities.

"The flexible light foundations had saved one hundred thousand dollars over the customary massive foundations. Now how could the building be made as light and flexible? I divided the building into sections about sixty feet long. This is the safe limit for temperature cracks in reinforced concrete in that climate. Wherever part met part I provided through joints.

"To insure stability I carried the floor and roof loads as a waiter carries his tray on his upraised arm and fingers. At the center all supports were centered under the loaded floor-slabs; balancing the load instead of gripping the load at the edges with the walls, as in the accepted manner. In any movement a load so carried would be safe. The waiter's tray balanced on his hand at the center is the cantilever in principle.

"This was done. This meant that the working principle of the cantilever would help determine the style of the structure. So the cantilever became the principal feature of the structure and a great factor in shaping its forms throughout as the floor-slabs came through the walls and extended into various balconies and overhangs.

"Tokyo buildings were top heavy. The exaggerated native roofs were covered deep with clay, and the heavy roof tiles laid on over the clay would come loose and slide down with deadly effect into the narrow streets crowded with terrified humanity.

"So the outer walls, spread thick and heavy at the base and tapering towards the top, were crowned there by a light roof covered with hand-worked sheet copper tiles. The light roof framing rested upon a concrete ceiling slab extended outward over the walls into an overhang, perforated to let sunlight into the windows of the rooms beneath.

"Now as to materials. What would be desirable and available? Again we go to the ground.

"A stone I had seen under foot and in common use in Tokyo building was a light, workable lava, called oya, weighing about as much as green oak and resembling travertine. It was quarried at Nikko and was floated down on rafts by sea to Tokyo and then by canal to the site. I liked this material for its character but soon found that the building committee, made up of the financial autocracy of the empire, considered it sacrilege to use a material so cheap and common for so dignified a purpose. But finally the building committee gave in and we bought our own quarries at Nikko. We used oya (the lava) throughout the work, combining it with concrete walls cast in layers within thin wall shells of slender bricks.

"Large or small, the pieces of lava could be easily hollowed out at the back and set up with the hollow side inside, as one side of the slab-forms for casting the concrete. In this way the three materials were cast solidly together as a structural unit when the concrete was poured into them.

"Copper, too, was a prominent feature in our list of available hand-worked materials.

"Thus the 'Teikoku' (Imperial Hotel) after these measures were taken became a jointed steel-reinforced monolith with a thin integral facing of lava and thin brick, the whole sheltered overhead by light copper tiles. The mass of the structure rests upon a kind of pincushion. The pins were set close enough together to support, by friction, the weight calculated to be placed upon them. To the lengthwise and cross-wise work in this particular structure all piping and wiring were made to conform. Both were designed to be laid in shafts and trenches free of construction. The pipes were of lead, sweeping with easy bend from trenches to shafts and curving again from shafts to fixtures. Thus any earthquake might rattle and flex the pipes as they hung but could break no connections. Last, but by no means least, an immense pool of water as an architectural feature of the extensive entrance court to the hotel was connected to its own private water system. This was to play its part in conflagration following in the wake of earthquake.

"During the execution of these ideas I found the language a barrier. Men and methods were strange. But the 'foreign' architect with twenty Japanese students from Tokyo and Kyoto University courses in architecture, some of whom were taken to Taliesin during the preliminary plan making, and one excellent American builder, Paul Mueller, made up the band that built the Imperial Hotel. Hayashi San, the general manager of the Imperial Hotel, was in direct charge of everything. The principal owner, the Imperial Household, was represented by Baron Okura. And there was a board of directors composed of five captains of Japanese big business—ships, tobacco, cement, and banking.

"The original plans which I had worked out at Taliesin for the construction I threw aside as educational experience for the architect only and worked out the details on the ground as we went along. Plans served only as a preliminary study for final construction.

"Those Japanese workmen! How clever they were. What skill and industry they displayed! So instead of trying to execute preconceived methods of execution, thereby wasting this precious human asset in vainly trying to make the workmen come our way, we learned from them and willingly went with them, their way. I modified many original intentions to make the most of what I now saw to be naturally theirs. But, of course, curious mistakes were common. I had occasion to learn that the characteristic Japanese approach to any subject is, by instinct, spiral. The Oriental instinct for attack in any direction is oblique or volute and becomes wearisome to a direct Occidental, whose instinct is frontal and whose approach is rectilinear.

"But, then, they made up for this seeming indirection by gentleness, loyalty, and skill. Soon we began to educate the 'foreigners' as they did us, and all went along together pretty well.

"As the countenance of their building began to emerge from seeming confusion the workmen grew more and more interested in it. It was a common sight to see groups of them intelligently admiring and criticizing some finished feature as it would emerge to view. There was warmth of interest and depth of appreciation, unknown to me in the building circles of our country in our own day, to prove the sincerity of their pleasure and interest in their work.

"Finally, out of this exercise of free will and common sense, with this unusual Western feeling of respect for the East and for Japanese life and traditions in view as discipline and inspiration, what would emerge?

"A great building is to be born; one not looking out of place where it is to stand across the park from the Imperial Palace. The noble surrounding walls of the Palace rose above the ancient moat. The gateways to the Palace grounds, guarded by blue-tiled, white-walled buildings nesting on the massive stone walls, were visible above the moat across the way. It was architecture perfect of its kind and as Japanese as the countenance of the race. I conceived the form of this new associate— the Imperial—as something squat and strong, as harmonious with this precedent as the pines in the park. It should be a form seen to be bracing itself against storm and expected temblor. Appeal has already been made to imagination in a realm scientific; but pure reason and science must now wait there at the doorstep.

"Wait there while something came to Japanese ground—something not Japanese, certainly, but sympathetic, embodying modern scientific building ideas by old methods not strange to Japan. No single form was really Japanese but the whole was informed by unity. The growing proportions were suitable to the best Japanese tradition. We have here in the individuality of the architect a sincere lover of old Japan, his hat in hand, seeking to contribute his share in the transition of a great old culture to a new and inevitably foreign one. Probably the new one was unsuitable. Certainly it was as yet but imperfectly understood by those who were blindly, even fatuously, accepting it as superior to their own. A great tragedy, it may be.

"Looking on then as now, it seemed to me as though tragedy it must be. The Far East had so little to learn from our great West, so much to lose where culture is concerned.

"I might ameliorate their loss by helping to make much that was

IMPERIAL HOTEL. EMPEROR'S ENTRANCE
"I HAVE SOMETIMES BEEN ASKED WHY I DID NOT MAKE THE OPUS MORE 'MODERN.' THE ANSWER
IS THAT THERE WAS A TRADITION THERE WORTHY OF RESPECT AND I FELT IT MY DUTY AS WELL
AS MY PRIVILEGE TO MAKE THE BUILDING BELONG TO THEM SO FAR AS I MIGHT. THE PRINCIPLE
OF FLEXIBILITY INSTEAD OF RIGIDITY HERE VINDICATED ITSELF WITH INSPIRING RESULTS."—
F. LL. W.

spiritually sound and beautiful in their own life, as they had known it so well, over into a pattern of the unknown new life they were so rashly entering. To realize this ambition in concrete form, apparent in a structure that acknowledged and consciously embodied this appropriate pattern, was what I intended to do in this masonry building 500 feet long by 300 feet wide. It was a world complete within itself. It now may be seen. It is known far and wide as it stands on the beaten path around the world. Said Baron Takahashi to a conscientious objector from America, 'You may not like our Imperial Hotel but we Japanese like it. We understand it.'

"Two years later—1923—in Los Angeles: news was shouted in the streets of awful disaster. Tokyo and nearby Yokohama were wiped out by the most terrific temblor in history. Appalling details came in day after day after the first silence when no details could be had. As the news began to add up it seemed that nothing human could have withstood the cataclysm.

"Too anxious to get any sleep I kept trying to get news of the fate of the New Imperial and of my friends, Shugio, Hayashi, Endo San, my boys and the Baron, hosts of friends I had left over there. Finally the third or fourth day after the first outcry, about two o'clock in the morning, the telephone bell. Mr. Hearst's *Examiner* wished to inform me that the Imperial Hotel was completely destroyed. My heart sank as I laughed at them. 'Read your dispatch,' I said. The *Examiner* read a long list of 'Imperial' this and 'Imperial' that.

"'You see how easy it is to get the Imperial Hotel mixed with other Imperials. If you print the destruction of the new Imperial Hotel as news you will have to retract. If anything is above ground in Tokyo it is that building,' I said, and hoped.

"Their turn to laugh while they spread the news of destruction with a photograph across the head of the front page in the morning. Then followed a week or more of anxiety. Conflicting reports came continually because during that time direct communication was cut off.

"Then—a cablegram.

FRANK LLOYD WRIGHT, OLIVE HILL RESIDENCE, HOLLY-
WOOD, CALIFORNIA.
FOLLOWING WIRELESS RECEIVED TODAY FROM TOKYO,
HOTEL STANDS UNDAMAGED AS MONUMENT TO YOUR
GENIUS HUNDREDS OF HOMELESS PROVIDED BY PERFECTLY
MAINTAINED SERVICE. CONGRATULATIONS.
OKURA.

"For once in a lifetime good news was newspaper news and the Baron's cablegram flashed around the world to herald what? To herald the triumph of good sense in the head of an architect tough enough to stick to it through thick and thin. Yes, that. But it was really a new approach to building, the ideal of an organic architecture at work, that really saved the Imperial Hotel.

"Both Tokyo houses of the Baron were gone. The splendid museum he gave to Tokyo was gone. The building by an American architect, whose hand he took to see him through, was what he had left in Tokyo standing intact, nor could love or money buy a share in it, now.

"When letters finally came through, friends were found to be safe. And it appeared that not one pane of glass was broken in the building— no one harmed. Neither was the plumbing or the heating system damaged at all. But something else was especially gratifying to me. After the first great quake was over, the dead lying in heaps, the Japanese came in droves, dragging their children into the courses and up onto the terraces of the building, praying for protection by the God that had protected the Teikoku. Then, as the wall of fire that follows every great quake came sweeping across the city toward the long front of the Imperial, driving a continuous wail of human misery before it, the Hotel boys formed a bucket line to the big pool of the central entrance court (the city mains were disrupted by the quake) and found there a reserve of water to keep the wood window frames and sash wet to meet the flames. The last thought for the safety of the Imperial had taken effect.

"Early in the twentieth century, a world in itself, true enough to its purpose and created spontaneously as any ever fashioned by the will of any creator of antiquity, had been completed within a sector of the lifetime of its one architect. Such work in ancient times generally proceeded from generation to generation and from architect to architect. Strange! Here expert handicraft had come at the beck and call of one who had, up to that time, devoted most of his effort to getting buildings true to modern machine processes built by machine.

"Here in the Far East a significant transition building was born. Are really good buildings all transition buildings? But for the quality of thought that built it, the ideal of an organic architecture, it would surely have been just 'another one of those things' and have been swept away.

67

IMPERIAL HOTEL. COURT

"While the New Imperial only partially realized the ideal of an organic architecture, the pursuit of that ideal made the building what it really was, and enabled it to do what it did do. The fact that were I to build it again it would be entirely different, although employing the same methods and means, does not vitiate my thesis here. It greatly strengthens it.

"Now let us glance at what followed this natural approach to the nature of a problem as a natural consequence. Opposition, of course, followed until finally Baron Okura took full responsibility and saw the building through. There was the unfriendly attitude of Americans and Englishmen. Though none too friendly to each other, they opposed this approach. They had owned Tokyo up to now because, where foreign culture was being so freely and thoughtlessly bought, they were best sellers. The Germans were there, strong too, but they were almost out of the running by now. My sympathetic attitude, Japan for the Japanese, was regarded as treason to American interests. I encouraged and sometimes taught the Japanese how to do the work on their building

IMPERIAL HOTEL. FROM
STAIRWAY TO GRAND BALL-
ROOM, VIEW TOWARD PEA-
COCK GALLERY BELOW.

themselves. The American construction companies were building ten-story steel buildings with such architecture as they had hung to the steel, setting the steel frames on long piles which they floated across the Pacific from Oregon and drove down to hard pan. I suppose they were built in this fashion so the steel might rattle the architecture off into the streets in any severe quake? These companies were especially virulent where I was concerned.

"The Western Society of American Engineers gratuitously warned me that my 'scheme for foundations was unsound.' The A.I.A.—American Institute of Architects—passing through Tokyo when the building was nearly finished, took notice and published articles in Tokyo papers declaring the work an insult to American architecture, notifying my clients, and the world generally, that the whole thing would be down in the first quake with horrible loss of life.

"Finally, when the building was about two-thirds completed, it came directly to the directors from such sources that their American architect was mad. Now every director except one (my sponsor, the

Baron), so worked upon continually for several years, became a spy. The walls had ears. Propaganda increased. General Manager Hayashi was 'on the spot.' My freedom was going fast and I worked on under difficulties greater than ever. Hayashi San, the powerful Okura, and my little band of Japanese student apprentices were loyal and we got ahead until the final storm broke in a dark scene in a directors' meeting. Then the Baron took over the reins himself to see me through with my work, and the building of the New Imperial went forward more smoothly to conclusion.

"I have learned that wherever reason shows its countenance and change is to take place, the reaction in any established order, itself not organic, is similar. Therefore organic architecture has this barrier to throw down or cross over or go around.

"As for government, I should say here that no permit to build the Imperial Hotel was ever issued by the government. I explained to the proper Imperial Department our intention, registered the drawings. The result was visitation by Japanese authorities, more explanations, head shakings. But the attitude was entirely friendly and sympathetic in contrast to the attitude that might be expected in our own country. Finally we were told no permit was needed, to go ahead, they would watch proceedings and hoped to learn something from the experiment. They could not say that most of the ideas did not seem right but, having no precedent, they could not officially act. They could wink, however, and 'wink' the government did.

"This 'wink' is the utmost official sanction organic architecture or any thought-built action of the sort in any medium may expect from a social order itself inorganic and in such danger of disturbance if radical examination is permitted that even an approach in that direction is cause for hysteria. Institutions such as ours are safe, in fact remain 'institutions' only upon some status quo, some supreme court, which inevitably becomes invalid as life goes on."

On his last return trip from Tokyo, an incident occurred that became imprinted forever in his mind. For years he told our friends the story of that last journey across the Pacific.

"Why don't you write it down?" I asked him one day. "It is a good story."

"I will," he said, and right then and there sat at his desk and wrote down the story which he could hardly wait to read to me:

"Crossing the Pacific on a little Japanese vessel, the Tamba Maru, there was a funeral at sea. The seventh day out a Japanese boy had died back there in the steerage. We, some thirty or more first-class passengers, stood above looking down from our promenade deck at a pathetic bundle, the body of the boy, sewed up in dingy sailcloth and laid out now on the hatch of the lower after-deck. Japanese seamen and Japanese passengers from second-class steerage, with folded arms and bared heads, crowded around the bundle, waiting. A little unpainted wooden tray, some prepared rice and fish upon it, stood at the feet of the boy—the little tray with fresh food being the Shinto rite or symbol of the solicitude of the living for the welfare of the dead in the long journey to the ancestors.

"Several missionaries were aboard. The little Japanese Captain all the way over had been most anxious to please his foreign passengers. So, thinking to pay his respects to us, the obliging little Captain politely asked a missionary—a pale-faced, white-eyed, full-beaked, full-bearded, Scotch strongman—to help consecrate this commitment of a land-loving human body to the great sea it must always have dreaded in life—the great inimical unknown.

"This stalwart Christian advocate, thus representing us, was standing there below among the little crowd of reverent countrymen of the dead boy. Just outside the cleared space, he loomed above the Japanese with the attitude of authority. The little Captain, standing by his dead, looked toward 'the man with a mission' and bowed to him to begin. The missionary, his stern face otherwise expressionless, pointed to the little tray of food, the Shinto token, and waved it overboard with the sweep of a stiff arm. Without moving from his spot, this fanatic repeated the offensive gesture, each time more haughtily than before.

"The little Captain, confused, looked towards his people, then up at us as though for rescue, then back again to the Christian. This several times.

"The appeal was in vain.

"The man of God repeated his haughty gesture several times. Our obliging little host saw the hopelessness of the situation, but still he hesitated. Shamed myself, I pitied the Captain as he walked over, hesitated, then abruptly lifted the little tray, carried it to the rail and dropped it overboard.

"There was no sound from the onlookers, nor movement among them as the little Japanese Captain stepped back so that the mighty parody of a Christian might now come forward. He condescended. Clearing his throat, he declared that the Captain had come to him and asked him to say a few words on this occasion and that, after making some careful inquiries among the boy's fellow passengers as to what sort of youth he was, he had found out that the boy had lived an honest enough sort of life so far as anybody knew. And so, notwithstanding certain religious scruples, he had consented to oblige the Captain. Then he proceeded arrogantly to expound his creed.

"At last he ended this appalling indignity imposed upon the helpless. A plank was pushed out over the rail in the name of God, and the canvas bundle that had been a boy, whose faith had been Shinto, was placed on it. The plank was tilted by the Japanese seamen and the small bundle slid down, plunged from the end of the plank down into the black sweeping waves. As we stood looking, it was soon lost to sight forever back there in elemental gloom.

"Then the 'holy man' with a mission made his way to the upper and Christian deck. As he reached us, no longer able to control my fury I swiftly seized him by the whiskered throat for one brief second, and then my friends held me back. . . . So there was but one human body consigned to the mercy of the deep that day—one perhaps alive in death. Another, safe enough on the ship, but securely dead—in life."

A NEW LIFE

After the great triumph of the Imperial Hotel and the building of the California houses in the early twenties, Frank Lloyd Wright returned to Chicago. At this time of his life he was alone and after the many years of struggle to bring his ideas into concrete form, having to fight every step of the way against entrenched forces everywhere organized to resist and obstruct the new, he was now at a low ebb. But providence usually comes to help those who live for an ideal. I was myself searching for an expression of life that placed the spirit above all else and it was then that we met, fell in love at first sight, married and stayed together for life.

In the autumn of 1925 we were well established at Taliesin in Wisconsin. On one of those lovely frosty mornings we were looking over his mail when he exclaimed, "See what I have! The Wendingen from Holland—the publication of my work." As we bent over the large, beautifully proportioned book, with its light cloth covers, he opened it slowly and there, after the first page, was the poetic portrait of him which has since been sealed in my memory of the first year of our life together.

"Look at this," he said, pointing to the inscription. It read: "Some Flowers to Frank Lloyd Wright."

74

FRANK LLOYD WRIGHT

GIVANNA LLOYD WRIGHT— PHOTOGRAPHS TAKEN ABOUT THE TIME OF THEIR FIRST MEETING

"And now," he added swiftly, "the bouquet is yours also."

The preface was written by the Dutch architect H. Th. Wijdeveld. "This is a fine piece of work," Mr. Wright said. "It is very well done indeed. Wijdeveld understands my architecture. I believe that Holland will go far along the line of architecture; it is there that the architects seem to have taken root in my work. Of course as usual it will never be on a large scale. And God forbid—because then I should feel I had become commonplace! But, spoofing aside, the enlightened minority does seem at this time to be strongest in Holland."

He had a warm feeling toward his friends there and his work was having an enormous influence in that country. I remember a letter he received from a friend saying: "All I see here is shades of you."

It has turned out that the volume which first gave him so much pleasure on that morning over forty years ago has since been universally recognized as one of the most important publications in the world of architecture.

As it happened, the first two major publications in recognition of Frank Lloyd Wright—that book and the recently republished *Buildings,*

TALIESIN, SPRING GREEN, WISCONSIN. "TALIESIN WAS THE NAME OF A WELSH POET, A DRUID-BARD WHO SANG TO WALES THE GLORIES OF FINE ART. LITERALLY, THE WELSH WORD MEANS 'SHINING BROW.' THIS HILL ON WHICH TALIESIN NOW STANDS AS 'BROW' WAS ONE OF MY FAVOR-ITE PLACES WHEN AS A BOY LOOKING FOR PASQUE FLOWERS I WENT THERE IN MARCH SUN WHILE SNOW STILL STREAKED THE HILLSIDE. THE BUILDINGS BECAME A BROW FOR THE HILL ITSELF."—
F.LL.W.

Plans and Designs, the Wasmuth portfolio—both originated in Europe, the continent where only the architecture of the past had had greatness.

Although, with the exception of the Imperial Hotel in Tokyo every building presented was designed by the master American architect for his native country, the impact of his work was first appreciated by Europeans, perhaps because of their hunger at the time for new, revolutionary forms.

America had had a fresh start, even if its early architectural expressions necessarily had to be imitative of Europe. Though for a long time culture came from abroad, the creative avant-garde in America began to be aware of the possibility of making a new world, and with time the American people at last realized the prophetic greatness of Frank Lloyd Wright, a native son. In the last ten years of his life, he enjoyed this recognition, knowing that his name and work had become known in every town and city in his own country as well as in every other civilized country of the world.

During the thirty-five years of my life with him, my husband kept the Wendingen edition close by his side. When he liked something very

TALIESIN. LIVING ROOM

much—a work of art, a vase, a piece of sculpture, a Japanese lacquer box, a Chinese painting—he would inevitably take it to his room. At times his room was so filled with art objects that I wondered how he could move about in it.

This book was always there. If it ever disappeared at any time, he would immediately say: "Who took my Wendingen? Bring that book back." Perhaps it was a sort of inspiration to him, a symbol of what he believed in. Sometimes he would say: "If I had to build that now, I would not use the same method. I would do it differently." And whenever he was asked what his favorite building was, he always said: "The next one." But when he looked over his past work he had great enjoyment in it, never criticism; and I believe the book often served as a relaxation for him to look through, for sometimes after he had been up late the night before, I would see it open on his desk in the morning.

He admired its proportions and layout and liked turning the pages, studying his buildings, reading the text; and he took great pleasure in the reproduction of his drawings and the splendid photographs. He would put it away for a time and a few days later pick it up again, always enjoying its beauty and often saying: "What a wonderful work this is." To him this was the book on architecture that would be good a hundred years from now; he believed it would have as much impact on the future as it has already had on the past.

I remember one day some thirty years later I found him with his friend and publisher Ben Raeburn sitting at ease and talking to one another about many things. Then Mr. Raeburn asked him: "Mr. Wright, since you like that book so much, how would you like me to publish it?" And Mr. Wright said: "Ben, that would be a noble work." And Ben Raeburn lived up to his promise. He published the book in as exquisite a form, and whenever I look through it now I receive the same living impression of his presence that I had on that day at Taliesin.

On that first morning, as we read the book together, turning its handsome, spacious pages and delighting in the illustrations of his buildings, the thought suddenly struck him: Perhaps Mr. Wijdeveld would be the man to come out and help rebuild the Hillside Home School. The buildings, which Mr. Wright had designed in 1902 for his aunts, stood on the Taliesin grounds a half mile or so from our house. They had been out of use for many years and now it was our dream to rebuild Hillside as a place for educating young architects. He felt this to be his duty to his aunts who had founded the coeducational school and his duty toward the future of architecture. He wrote to Holland.

Mr. Wijdeveld made the trip to Taliesin and after they shook hands Mr. Wright said, "Well, Wijdeveld, the best thing you could have done is this book—the Wendingen. That counts you *one!* It doesn't matter how many errors you commit now, that will always count you one. Your book brought you over here. If such understanding is yours I think you can help the work here that Olgivanna and I wish to organize. Maybe you can be the director of the school."

The next day we walked over to Hillside. It was in a pitiful state, ceilings and floors caving in, ruined by vandalism. We stood looking at it all, and the spirit of Mr. Wijdeveld visibly collapsed within him.

"This place is too far gone," he said. "You can do nothing to save it. It will take enormous capital to restore these buildings and far too much work."

But Mr. Wright did not think so. "It looks worse than it is," he said. "We can fix it up in no time. You bring your family over and we will all work on it together."

Mr. Wijdeveld thought it over. He did not see the great future which stood waiting for us to work on. "I cannot do it," he said. "I cannot bring my family, to burden them with such an enormous task. It is insurmountable."

Hillside did look terrible; it did need a superhuman effort to bring it back to life. Besides, this was a foreign country to him and, as he told me, it would be especially difficult for his family, accustomed to fine theatres, symphony concerts, and all the cultural attractions of a European city. This kind of change did present a grim picture.

After long consideration, measuring all the circumstances involved, Mr. Wijdeveld decided to give up his truly sincere desire to work alongside my husband. Sad and regretful, he finally sailed back to his native Holland.

We both were disappointed not to have Mr. Wijdeveld at Taliesin and we missed his cheerful spirit for quite some time.

But now Mr. Wright and I began to clean the buildings with our own hands—making order out of chaos. Every day we walked over to Hillside and attacked the work with more zest than ever. His spirit was indomitable and I raced fast to keep up with him. With hammer and nails almost constantly in his hands, he nailed the splitting boards together, repairing, patching, reorganizing, redesigning, changing the old gymnasium into a theatre, the carpenter shop into a dining room, and working on and on, until an opportunity came to employ a few workmen to help in the resurrection of Hillside. Somehow or other with that small handful of men, we managed to prepare the Hillside dining room and kitchen, but it was impossible to build any rooms as yet.

"Olgivanna, I know what we'll do," Mr. Wright said one day at Hillside. "We can still open our school; we will call it the Taliesin Fellowship and we will make our thesis for the apprentices the building of the drafting room. We'll start from the foundation up. We'll send the boys to get sand from the river banks; we'll send them to cut green lumber and quarry and haul rocks. We have a wonderful stone quarry in the valley near Pleasant Ridge. We'll have men come and saw the lumber right here. They will learn to be better architects than anywhere else in the world."

I responded to the idea immediately but I asked: "Where would they sleep?"

"Oh, that doesn't matter. We'll crowd them in at first. We'll manage it."

"All right," I said, "we'll manage it."

That very afternoon we returned to Taliesin and sat down to make plans for the rooms. It appeared that eventually we could actually house twenty-three people and even then we began to distribute them to the invisible students to come. I became very enthusiastic and started quickly to get the rooms ready. We got some of our faithful old carpenters William Weston and Ralph Reilly and our masons Charlie Curtis and Allan Brunker to make repairs here and there.

Mr. Wright and I outlined the complete education of an architect so that a student could be acquainted with all fields of architectural design by way of the direct experience which would enrich his psyche. Participation in the theatre at Taliesin would encompass music, choir, drama, dance, all to enter the architect's experience as an integral part of his life. We believed that knowledge of music should be part of his architectural training; love of music would give him a strand of inspiration in yet another direction. An architect should also be able to speak and write well, capable of describing an idea clearly and concisely, and so he would develop understanding of theatre and literature as well—

all to become part of his life. This was a great new concept of education for an architect, now to be materialized. With the rooms only half-finished we sent the first circulars out. Neither of us expected more than fifteen or so to respond, if that many to begin with.

On the fifteenth of September, 1932, car after car drove up to Taliesin. For the first time I saw my husband a little embarrassed, not quite knowing whether he should interview them all together or individually. "Maybe you had better interview them one by one," I suggested. As the young students came up, Carl Jensen, our secretary at that time, ushered them into the Taliesin studio at first, then into the loggia. While we were interviewing them, one young man strayed into the living room. I was just about to go out into the garden when I noticed him by the window; he had evidently been standing there for a long time. "And you?" I asked.

"Well," he said shyly, "I've been waiting here for some time. My name is Edgar Tafel."

"Oh, you have been forgotten. I will tell Mr. Wright."

After the interview, Mr. Wright said to me, "That young man is very good looking, isn't he? Like a curly-headed cherub."

"Yes," I said, "very nice looking indeed." We found out later that the shy cherub was in reality an incorrigible prankster.

As the days went on, twenty-three students gathered at Taliesin within a week. The windows were not in yet, nor were the doors, but fortunately the weather was warm. One day as I was looking from the bridge connecting the big kitchen with the living quarters, down in the court below I saw a tall young man carrying a door from our part of the house towards an apartment on the nearby hill. Not remembering his name, I called out: "Wait a minute, wait a minute. What are you doing with that door?"

"I have no door in my room, Mrs. Wright. I have taken this one from the guest wing below. I will pay for it."

"You take that door right back," I said. "And hang it where you took it from. It won't hurt you to be without a door for one day. We will have them all in by tomorrow." That young man turned out to be William Wesley Peters, who is now Chief Architect of the Taliesin firm.

The haphazard beginnings were as exciting to the young people as they were to us, and they blended with our spirit in this obviously new adventure in education. We had no knowledge as to how much money was needed to take care of healthy, rambunctious boys and girls. The tuition was $650.00 for a complete year of living, working, eating and studying, with only two weeks vacation. It never occurred to either of us that we might not be able to meet the requirements of financing this enterprise, but our spirit was so undaunted that it melted all physical obstructions in our way. From the beginning, our situation with automobiles at that time being rather poor, we sent one of the boys to buy groceries because he had a car, and the boys and girls worked everywhere, scrubbing floors, plastering, building shelves in their rooms. They were so filled with the energy we passed on to them that the Taliesin Fellowship was like a rocket, breaking all barriers.

The work we did was enormous. We organized everything in the same spontaneous way from day to day. When our hired cook became burdened with too much work, one of the students offered to help, and the Fellowship grew as naturally as our oak trees grew on the Taliesin hill. Little by little the jobs took shape, the pattern of life was forming, the first exciting days, weeks and months began to fall into a definite system of work and study.

The next year found us a fully going institution. As the years moved on we organized evenings in our Taliesin living room. Edgar Tafel played the piano, our daughter Svetlana played the violin, and we invited artists who came to Madison to give concerts. The most memorable of them at the time was the famous contralto, the late Sophie Breslau, whose accompanist was my friend, Ina Rublova. After her concert in Madison, Sophie Breslau came to Taliesin and sang for us until two in the morning.

Our work went on—always expanding. The big drafting room at Hillside was being built as we planned. Some of the boys went to cut lumber. Those who liked to quarry stones went down to the nearby quarry and loaded the truck with rocks. Those who loved to work with the large saw assisted the workmen at Hillside. Some helped in the kitchen, in the vegetable garden, in flower gardens; others planted trees. Some walked in the fields behind the harrow drawn by a team of horses, sowing oats, wheat and soybeans. New lawns were seeded everywhere, and the capacious new drafting room was added to the Hillside buildings. The whole great idea began to grow in incredible proportions, moving on, widening its radius. After a few years we decided that the number of apprentices must not get any larger lest

HILLSIDE. DRAFTING ROOM

we lose direct contact with the young people; forty was our limit, but we finally let it reach sixty. Even now I am still trying to keep it limited, but it is hard to refuse aspiring architectural students and sometimes I weaken and accept them though our numbers have now grown to eighty.

From those early years I remember an incident which exemplifies the natural courage that was one of Frank Lloyd Wright's most prominent attributes throughout his life, and that was also, I am sure, due in part to the source which issued from the rocks and mountains of Wales. He believed in cultivating everything in Taliesin that would make us self-supporting, so that if we were cut off at any time from civilization

HILLSIDE, SPRING GREEN, WISCONSIN

we could still function perfectly. He insisted on having our own electric plant, so we installed a Kohler generator at the first dam which he built to beautify the grounds, and it came into use for lighting all the buildings at Taliesin. Alternately the students as part of their daily work had to rise as early as five in the morning to turn on the hydro. It was a hard task, but an adventure.

Late one evening a young student could not turn the wheel because an important part of the engine had fallen into the pond. It was quite deep in that spot, about six feet of water, and the November evening was fiercely cold. Mr. Wright walked down the hill to the plant with three of our young men. "Well, which one of you will go into the water and pick up the part?" he asked. They looked at one another, shrugged their shoulders, and one of them demurred: "Well, Mr. Wright, I really don't think we should go into that water. It's icy, I don't want to catch pneumonia. The others don't seem to feel like it either."

"The idea!" replied Mr. Wright. "And you boys are supposed to be young!" He sat down on the bank, took off his shoes and socks, stripped off his coat, threw down his hat, and plunged into the water. He found the lost part, pulled it up out of the muddy creek bed, and came out shivering. "Here, put it back in now. At least that won't give you pneumonia! Come on, all of you, get at it!"

He climbed fast up the Taliesin hill and entered the house breathless. "I am frozen, Olgivanna, I'm frozen to the bone! Quick, some whisky and a hot bath." As he sat later in his chair by the fireplace, he could not get over the fact that those strong young people had seemed cowardly. "How can it be?" he asked. "I'm surprised. All you had to do was take off your shoes and coat and get into the water. That can't hurt anyone. They're old men, those fellows, that's what they are. I never ask anybody to do anything I wouldn't do." He didn't catch pneumonia or even the slightest cold. What to him was a natural act was to the three young men an incredible feat; even in later years when they talked about it they could not comprehend it; and he never understood why they had no "simple courage."

ARCHITECTURE AND EDUCATION

My husband and I rose early every morning with religious adherence. We always had breakfast together and no matter what we discussed, whether it was a radio talk we had heard, or music, architecture or philosophy, inevitably our conversation was exciting, but I often noticed that he would suddenly become restless; the familiar gleam would appear in his eyes, the sign of a new idea being generated in his mind. In order not to lose it, he would rise abruptly from his chair, putting on his hat and cape. "Well, I have to go now," he would say, moving swiftly. "I've got to go over to the drafting room and work," and I would watch him walk away with a graceful stride, his cape flowing with his motion.

He was always meticulous in his personal appearance, wearing immaculately tailored suits, capes and coats which he took extreme care to have made according to his own standards of style, elegant, graceful and, most of all, appropriate.

"We all know the feeling we have when we are well-dressed," he wrote, "and like the consciousness that results from it. It affects our conduct and you should have the same feeling regarding the home you live in. It has a salutary effect morally, to put it on a lower plane than it deserves, but there are higher results above that sure one. If you feel yourself becomingly housed, know that you are living according to the higher demands of a good society and of your own conscience, then you are free from embarrassment and not poor in spirit, but rich—in the right way. I have always believed in being careful about my clothes; getting well-dressed because I could then forget all about them."

Young people who were close to him naturally were influenced by him in more than one way; they drank freely from the source and could not help but be nourished by it.

To me he was, of course, direct and frank about this, as about everything else, and I could wear only the clothes he liked and often chose for me. An incident about this has stayed in my memory: It was, as it still is today, a Taliesin tradition to go out on picnics whenever possible on Saturdays or Sundays to explore new and unknown places. It happened one day that everyone was ready to leave except me. I was running towards the driveway when my husband, standing beside a car, took one look at me and said: "Do you realize you are going to a picnic?"

"Why yes."

"Then why do you look so drab? Go back and put something color-ful on. You don't look fit for a picnic. I want to see you in the countryside in something gay and lovely. Go on. We will wait."

It was a soft, sunny mid-day. I went back in a great hurry and changed my dress, put on a brilliant, colored scarf, took a red parasol and a broad-brimmed hat, and rushed back breathless. He smiled: "Good, now you look like somebody who is fit to go on a picnic."

He never took anything for granted. An idea which might have originated from some remote source, even a political talk we might have discussed, would eventually present itself in the form of a drawing to him. It was not necessarily the thought itself, but the energy pro-duced by it that worked in him; he did his work in designing with a power that was unceasing.

The utilitarian in architecture was for him a consequence of an original idea; he believed that if a building is truly beautiful it is bound to be practical—an organically beautiful building could never be im-practical—and he denounced buildings designed merely as "machines for living," declaring that they were ugly because they were motivated merely by expediency.

His morning work in the drafting room was of intense concentration. He loved the mornings of his life best, the times that were marked with the most productive activity, and liked to be stimulated then by opposing thoughts which could stir him to produce still more varied forms. In our life together there was some element that fortunately always enabled me to stimulate his thought and set his energy into action.

When he had given concrete form to a concept in his mind, he would immediately put it down on the drafting board. Usually the students would stand over him and watch him design, and after he had

finished his drawing he would sit down in turn at each student's drafting table to see what he was doing, making suggestions, indicating necessary changes. Imparting his thought directly to his students at the right time, he was a splendid teacher. Often he would lean over the drafting board of a young man and then, becoming interested in the drawing, would sit down. "This is very good, you know, this is very good, but . . ." meanwhile erasing practically all of the drawing while the poor student stood there, not quite knowing what was happening. Then he would say again: "It is all right. It is still good. The idea was good," and in the process of changing the drawing he had indicated the architect's future direction.

The human element was more important to him than architectural talent and what he appreciated most in a student was a sense of personal responsibility. He felt that a student's coming to Taliesin implied dissatisfaction with the orthodox teaching of architecture and did not believe that anyone could learn architecture by theory alone and, assuming that the student was a man of greater ability than those who had taught him, he proceeded to watch for character, which to him was most important. Of course he naturally liked to have a student who showed technical ability, and he admired a clean worker, one who always tidied up after himself. We worked together to develop the student's ethical sense; as a teacher he did so spontaneously, accomplishing it at precisely the right moment with a significant remark which later brought the desired results.

He called architecture "the mother art" but he was devoted to all the arts and crafts as well, believing them to be important components of architecture, and if a student showed ability along any of the outbranchings from the central core of architecture, he appreciated it and helped it grow. If, for instance, a young man was gifted in cabinet-making and carpentry, or had a way with flowers or plants, he invariably extolled the quality of his work.

He put strong emphasis on having the students present their designs so that we might evaluate their progress. They placed them in a large wooden box, designed and executed by one of them, and the event customarily took place at Christmas and on his birthday in June, usually in the morning. First of all Mr. Wright would examine and admire the box which was, and still is, made by a different student each year. He would look at it in various lights, touch it to feel its surface, remove the top and turn it over, remarking on the workmanship and, if it was well done, praising its proportions. He seemed to be as interested in the box as in its contents. On these occasions the young people would show how much they had grown, how well they had absorbed the idea of organic architecture by way of their own creative design. Each student designed a building—an office, a shopping center, a house, a church, a room—or interior furnishings. He left the choice to them. Throughout all the years of the Fellowship, I listened to the invaluable criticism, which he dealt rather gently. He was never too harsh a critic because he understood that the young people presented their very best; even if it was poor, he never discarded a design.

Now we continue this tradition after his death: twice a year we have an exhibition of drawings and, as before, one young man builds the box which in itself is often a work of art. When a drawing is presented to me and I see something remiss in it, I take the approach that I absorbed from him, trying to give the quality of judgment and criticism that will help the student evolve in a new direction so that he does not become submerged in a cliché. Mr. Wright and I both believed that the cliché is the worst enemy of a creative man. Even if we create an original form it can become a cliché from too frequent use, unless we grow to bring freshness of expression into whatever we do.

Today in the Frank Lloyd Wright School of Architecture we teach the techniques of drafting as he taught them. If a student has had no drafting experience, he learns first by tracing so that he may develop a free swing of his hand; in the second stage he is given some simple drawing to do; later he is assigned more complicated drafting, and then working drawings for an actual building. Because we are constantly building at Taliesin and shall continue to build for fifty or a hundred years, we are able to put students to work at drawings that we can correct. Never at any time do they have merely theoretical teaching; their technique is developed naturally. Mr. Wright often admonished a young man when looking at his drawing: "Your technique is bad, your lettering is bad. Your lettering must be perfect before you can ever draw a line." He demanded clean lines in everything. When the students, exercising their imagination in a concept of a house, presented drawings he would emphasize the importance of site, its relation to the environment, its purpose, the clients, the conditions of climate in the area, all the necessary considerations, giving them enough instruction at one time to enable them to continue on the same drawings for weeks afterwards. The technique, he often stated, will follow so long as the student knows what he is about.

The student first had Mr. Wright's criticism, then that of Mr. Wright's assistants, who are now qualified to teach the principles of organic architecture. A student is required to produce his own form in accordance with the purpose which it is to serve and, with conditions constantly changing and new materials becoming available, he has to apply himself and change accordingly, always building on the principle that a building should belong to its terrain and its purpose, whether in city or country, because its effects in the community of which it will be a part are lasting.

Mr. Wright encouraged every possibility of development. If a student had some knowledge of music, he would inspire him to widen his knowledge by having him participate in our Sunday concerts; and if an applicant knew something about plumbing or electricity, he believed that if we put him to work in that field he would be absorbing the sense of architectural forms just as well as when drafting. This was difficult for people to understand at first, but they very soon began to take pride in whatever work was at hand.

He was completely open to any good suggestion and had an extraordinary power of absorption. He often asked, concerning a design of his own, "What do you think now, boys? We are up against this problem here, how can we solve it?" and when he heard a sensible idea he would apply it immediately. He would often ask me to come to the drafting room to see a drawing; I was the last and, of course, the most severe critic. He knew that. I was frank to tell him if I thought something could be changed; at times he burst out angrily: "You know nothing. How can you declare yourself, what do you know about architecture, anyway?"

"Why did you ask me then? You brought me here. You asked me what I thought of it." And I was often told later that he had made those very changes in the drawing which I had suggested.

After concentrated work in the drafting room he usually went to the office where his right hand man and secretary, the late Eugene Masselink, a fine painter who worshipped Mr. Wright, had prepared work for him. That was the time in which he corresponded and frequently wrote articles or worked on a new book.

Telephone calls often interrupted, but he never refused them; he was easy to contact and transacted a great deal of business on the phone efficiently and quickly. He knew precisely what he was going to say and in solving a problem made his statement so concisely that there was no question about how to proceed after he had given instructions.

In the same way, he did not believe in long letters; his were brief and to the point. Whenever he wrote a letter in anger he said: "I should not have done it. I did it only because I was angry, and whenever I am angry I write a long letter and that means it is no good." There were times, however, when his letters provoked people, so I asked him to read them to me before mailing them off. If my reaction was negative he would say: "Too bad, I had such a good time doing it and I think it is a good letter. Well, I got it out of my system anyway. All right, all right, I won't send it this time." But many a time he did send it and inevitably regretted it.

"I give this advice to all of you," he would counsel our young people, "write your letter in the evening and destroy it in the morning. You will get it out of your system and you will not have offended anyone. When you think over certain things that have happened in your life, you will see that they are less important than you thought they were in the moment of anger."

He liked to say that he hated people to confide in him because they put a burden on him. "Do not give me any confidential matter," he often said, "because I am not going to keep it to myself, to encumber my mind with it." Consequently no one spoke to him of personal problems. He was a man whom people asked about architecture, philosophy, painting or sculpture, questions creative or entirely impersonal, yet he said that the only things that interested anybody were strictly personal in nature. When he was accused at an Air Force Academy meeting of involving personalities by bringing in the name of a certain architect whose work he did not admire, he answered that the only things that concern anybody are personal matters. These strange contradictions or counter-positions of thought seemed to balance themselves in him; he had many personal and companionable relationships with our young people

Every Sunday morning after breakfast he gave talks in the Fellowship dining room. As he often said, it was a way of keeping himself at a definite point in space and time where he chose to be. He had many such points in space and time, but the Sunday morning talk was among his favorites. He would speak to the Fellowship on some subject that had arisen in his mind that particular morning or about something he had read or he might answer a question he had been asked previously.

He liked to illustrate the theory of learning at Taliesin with the story of the bee in Oklahoma: "A man once decided to get beehives. One day, noticing that things were slack, he picked up a bee on his finger and said to it, 'Bee, look around you—here is Oklahoma and if you can't make good honey you're a hell of a bee!' Here is Taliesin, here is work, here is inspiration, here is the source, and if you can't make a good architect out of yourself, something is wrong with you."

He always felt that the message he delivered to the young architects would prove to be important to their future as well as to their lives in the present, and took his talks extremely seriously, whether he addressed them to few or many. His resources were endless; during the years of his talks to the Fellowship he explored many subjects besides architecture: politics, economics, painting, science, religion, all the concerns that make up our interior structure. It was of course a form of teaching, to be listened to carefully and acted upon, and because he believed that their attention was best in the morning before the start of the day, he gave the talks to the students one morning a week only. His talks were comprehensive expositions of thought in action; he never rushed them, delivering them in a meditative way so that they could be received with ease by young people. The direction he gave them was always towards a better architecture, painting, sculpture, poetry—a better society. He was constantly advising them to read the great authors of the world, and often read aloud to them. Naturally each one received and absorbed according to his capacity and tried to put into action the ideas to which he had listened. It was a real class, but he would have objected to its being called a class. He never wanted to be considered a professional and insisted that his work was that of an amateur. "If you are a professional," he said, "you are dead; if you are an expert, you should be buried."

Because he had no use for a mechanical order repeated for days to months to years, he would often change the pattern of his day, provided it fit into his work in architecture. The joy of the little boy playing with sand and branches and stone he transformed into his life's work. But his work was demanding, and he would often come to me exhausted:

"Oh, so many decisions upon decisions I have to make. I am tired, Olgivanna." He would sit down but his "rest" was short-lived, often only for a few minutes. Some sight, perhaps the landscape, moving and alive with cloud shadows, or a hibiscus flower that had just bloomed in a flash of scarlet or the beauty of a bird in flight, stimulated him with new energy which drove him directly back to the drafting room. He had that kind of communion with nature. His appreciation was never merely theoretical, intellectual or analytical; it was ever-present and effortless. I trace this back to his childhood years of hardship and his exuberant love of the world around him. Every facet of a natural form was an inspiring circumstance to him. Affected first by its beauty in a spontaneous impact, he then drew knowledge which gave him insight into the very spirit of the form he had studied.

One Sunday morning he showed a tray of sea shells to the Taliesin Fellowship and spoke to them on "housing" in nature:

"I wish to give you a little lesson in housing. I will try to show you what 'housing' in Nature amounts to—and if you really want to study housing, what a good place it is to go to study. To think that there is but one issue, *the* issue, to be found in any generic principle of Nature is, of course, merely current political and academic confusion of ideas.

Given the cold dissector we call 'science' and the credit which we now accord it, it is likely to codify and administer all life. Perhaps science derives rules of measurement from life, a life which then becomes: just how much and how far and in what direction, by how much or by whom or when it is to be lived. The making of such codes, though needed, even by a democratic civilization, should not become a habit-of-mind. But if the creation of a good free life for all is our aim, such codes must change as organic changes occur. Opportunity to function for the greatest good of the most deserving is the end and aim of genuine democratic authority. Only in the light of that kind of interpretation is science indispensable. I believe, however, that science has already so far overshot its humane value to us at the moment that we need to 'catch up' with the new tools science has already put into our new tool box, though the answer now seems to be 'more tools.' Nor do I think this catching up can be done if we depend on science or instinct (the subjective mind we call 'taste') to do so. There is something more now needed in the middle-ground of our American lives. There is something missing there now in the way of knowledge, which we do not have; or if we have it, do not apply it. What that something is, is what we as architects would like to learn.

"What have we as architects missed? I should say it is great art and a true religion. If the day ever dawns when science, art and religion become as one by recognizing each other's facilities and qualities as different in reality, but really as reinforcing each other, we would then have something like the thing which is now missing.

"And now let us turn, carefully, critically, to these hundreds of beautiful, infinitely varied little creature-houses which I have here under my hands—sea homes. Here, you see, is natural housing. Is it on a lower level than ours? In a sense that is true, but is not the humble housing of these lower creature-forms of life which you see here marvelous manifestation of fertile organic process? Now where in all this bewildering world of organic form in which we live and function is the motive, the impulse, the idea? Here we will see that idea. Just one idea in all of them? Yes, but where is there the least limitation to variety?

"Now, speaking of human housing, here are excellent lessons for young architects. For instance, if the human mind is so limited that it can only take in the beauty and fitness of some special one of these shells, if we really want to develop a culture of our own so that we can perform similar 'miracles,' then we need to see in what we are deficient and must inform ourselves, so as not to have to submit to limitations by broker or code or formula for designs for houses, or in the name of science submit to some blind official authority all of our human performances when we attempt to house ourselves. A living death is ours in what we do, as compared with what is seen here in the work of these little creature-natures. Here we see in the housing of this lowly life of the sea the nature housing which is doing exactly the thing we seem to lack: living in naturally inspired, beautiful form. See the innate quality of invention in this collection of small houses by hundreds of small *natural* beings. They each built their own houses in a beautiful, consistent variation which is never finished. Creation is here seen going on and on, forever. Here is no question of privilege or degree; all is a matter of natural *principle* at work on *natural design*. Such multitudinous expression as this should indicate what design might mean to us were we to be similarly inspired.

"There is no good reason why our dwelling-places, the 'housing' which we so recklessly perpetrate, should be all alike all over this country. Why should not our houses be quite as fertile and consistent in the consequences of imaginative resource in design as we see here in these little sea-houses? Why do we need take any one expression of formula, carry it out to a dead end and execute it as though that were our all, stultified by our own stupidity? Are we cashiered by our own cupidity? Here in this collection of little 'houses' is one of the most inspiring lessons you could possibly find. So study these shells to see that, although there is but *one* generic principle in all of them and all these little houses are doing the same thing to the same end, they are not doing it in the same way. Nature's most beloved asset, individuality, proceeds here and succeeds. This clamshell, for instance, is based on the opening and shutting of the house—halves hinged. Are clams, being more mechanical and less ornamental, of a higher development or, being less mechanical and more ornamental, are these others inferior?

"Can you see how all these significantly concordant shapes and ornamental lines, forms and designs in all these bright, varied colors and textures, are tributary, obedient to forces exerted upon their lives from within? Each shell has been 'designed.' Each pattern of ornamentation that we see here is never less than appropriate. That is to say that every

ARCHITECTONICA MAXIMA (SUNDIAL)

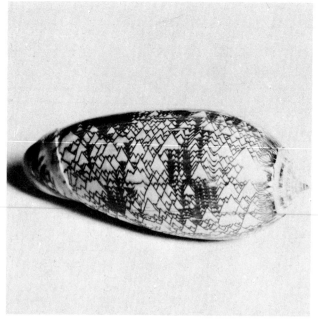

OLIVA MAURITIANA

pattern you see is, and the exquisite forms of the shells themselves are, all the consequence of innate obedience to forces exerted upon the shell-ship from within as the shell itself is formed. A vast city is ultimately being made.

"Probably this particular small being grew in a coral bed, where the very shape and every feature of the house was necessary to the preservation of its life under existing circumstances, keeping its inhabitant from being destroyed by alien forces. That is true, generally, of all these more inclusive, more highly developed, cellular designs. Now see this extraordinary fantasy! Here is an original, saying exactly the same thing as are all the others, saying it but with infinitely more variable form at much greater expense of work and material. All the 'houses' eventually harmonize because of obedience to principle. Here you may see what individuality might mean to us in the architecture of a nation like ours, a democracy, if we were similarly inspired by principle. If you want a lesson in organic structure, wherein what we call ornament is a suitable sequence and consequence of form and method, here it is. What enjoyable coloration! What beautiful texturing and color! These natural houses are little poems. One sees the ebb and flow, the plasticity of the elements of the sea in which it lives; and by way of its currents and incidental pressures under and in which all came to exist, these now appear as shells. All is therefore natural as we can see. These little sea houses are lovely, and in no mean way. Beautiful? Yes, all of them. Not one fails to express principle, the one that gave it birth as it governs all birth. Some of the creatures seem still young, growing up. Perhaps a new species is in the becoming.

"You see now a beautiful instance of 'such as the life is, such is the form.' Varied natural consequences of principle are seen in the finished work. Every single shell comes into its own and to a different conclusion in its effects, however it may start or whatever the ultimate may be. Every little maker has developed true individuality. See this amazing variety of means to end. When you get the simple secret governing the inner life and shaping of this sea-shell and you learn why that thing is what it is, how a certain common aim does persist in the over-all result of the various forms of this sea-life as in any other type of natural life, that will mean that you have the secret of characteristic differences in housing that might apply to the human family. If you are more aware of Nature differences that mean the various races and their peoples you will command a true, inspiring dissidence. See the seemingly utter differences harmoniously existing between these shells. Yet what is there in common? In these internally reinforced shells, structure is due to a scarcity of raw materials. Here we see the economical webs of the

CHAMBERED NAUTILUS, SECTIONS

reinforcing rib instead of the thicker, heavier wall-mass of outer wall-bearing patterns, but pattern in all seemingly predestined to obey purpose. Observe the children of movement, movement within and without that of the creature within and without, that of the sea and drifting sands impelled by wave and tide in which it grew. Why can we not be as fertile and rational in our work as architects for human beings on earth? Where but to Nature herself can we go to study this obedience to the inner forces that may be significant and have such wide but harmonious consequences in our lives?

"Look at this little house, probably accorded the work of a genius in the species. These are homes, 'naturized buildings.' Shall we call each a different idea? No, they are not different in idea. But that idea is generic and so productive that this infinite variety of expression of that one idea comes naturally into life. This variety can go on forever, and does. Yes, it is infinite. That is why I show you these little manifestations as 'housing.' Opportunity for individual expression develops these forms by way of changes not only of material, environment and shape, but also of movement in environment. All such life-changes are here recorded by expression in form. It makes one feel pretty stupid to see this beautiful instance of exquisite variety in these humble creatures of the sea when we see government housing or, for instance, a Levittown. We sit down to our drafting boards and try to do something, but nothing like this comes until we too are similarly imbued with principle and so become sufficiently masters of our own lives to guide others.

"Finally, what is the element in Nature which produces, on principle, notwithstanding all limitations, such fascinating, rich, harmonious individualities? Is not this the God in them? It is the same element that produces the differences in human beings, of the same or different races, differing individualities within the differences of the races. Yes, it is all the same. All are armed in their particular way against destruction. But what is the magic secret of the appropriate forms, from within, of them all? This is the major question you should all study as artists. The answer is written in the great book of creation in which you may some day have a page of your own Nature. Because there, in principle of Nature, is where the artist may find light on what he here sees and feels.

"Abstraction of principle—an expression of inner life by means of appropriate obedience to principle—is really your field. Is there a *mind,* would you say, governing, producing, these infinite changes of form, these varieties of single species in Nature? The lower the form of life, the greater the necessity for the armament we see here. So is it a matter of mind? Why is beauty being done? Science can investigate and take it all apart, but it comes against a barrier no science can ever penetrate. What this inner life is, we do not, cannot, know. You have heard the story of the little boy who cut out the head of his drum to see where the sound came from? Science would be that little boy. But this innate source of beauty in expression is what should inspire us all, give us faith in our own divinity—if that is the proper word to use for such inspiration where we would be concerned.

"You see, there is never a limit. Nothing indicates that the thing could end so long as the principle, inviolate, is in motion. Nevertheless, civilization like ours comes in the rough and says, 'Let's get on with this, let's get an easy pattern out of it all, so we can stamp it all out just the same, let's put this thing into production.' Then comes the cliché—a 'style'—and the divine element of Style goes out. The only divine quality in us vanishes. Our realtors, national housers, our bureaucracy, have become an atrocious liability, a negative materiality of no great value to our American culture except as makers of commonplace breeding-stables, entirely without the morality of beauty because those who make them have no sense at all of God, of the beautiful.

"A sense of God must have reached these little lives to perform this rich, innate beauty of form. Just as there must be a divine sense in us, unfortunately slumbering now, there is in us too the interior sense of becoming which we can only call Principle or call God—a true senti-ment ready to awaken to housing us all, and which you will eventually see has infinite capacity no human mind can ever completely encom-pass, ever exhaust, imprison or extinguish. Here you see humble but innate evidence. If man awakens in architecture to the human phases of what we call our divinity, an inherent element will awaken and be at work in all of life. Then and there you may find the secret of conform-ing to this eternal Idea. Therein lies the value of these exquisite little 'buildings' of the sea to us as we live on earth, if we study their evidence as artists should study. Here, in this feature of Nature, is one page for the architect's 'school-book.'

"Let us for a moment study the coral family. Another family entirely, but as fascinating because the same innate principle is working in this coral-branch, though in totally different schemes. Yet, the Idea is the same. Some of the coral-branches will grow up in the water as great long fingers, or spears, and wave to and fro with the movements of the water, all on a little hinge. By proper pressure at proper times, they become detached and float away to find another hinge. The whole process repeats over and over again. In all of this, there is an element of becoming. The circumstances are always determining the shape of all variable forms. Form develops and travels accordingly.

"This certain, common tendency throughout all Nature serves to unite creation. Nature's work is harmonious by nature, all through different species and forms. In us all there is exactly this same principle secretly working all the time but obscured by artificiality. Now what would our human divinity be? Certainly divinity, principle, God, is manifest here in the beauty of this minor form of life. Then, how about us in this our highest form of life ever known, as we like to say? What, without this innate development from within, will become of us all? Is science and civilization killing our natural divinity instead of developing it? What end readly are we now pursuing? What is civilization without this innate culture according to inner principle developing harmonious form in us and among us? What are we? What God do we worship?

"Manifestly, Nature loves and continually seeks such individuality as this. Nature places her premium upon it, resists and punishes the loss of it in the great fields of her glorious creation. If our artificial civilization as a way of life goes contrary to this divinity and does not learn the nature of it, does not learn secrets of becoming behavior and appropriate character, does not know the necessary change of form, then what is going to happen to us? Where are we going? Something is going to hit us, or we are eventually going to hit something hard. What has already struck at us? Is the time for us now as architects to learn to say wherein lies salvation for us as human beings in this our amazing scientific civilization trying to live without art? Is the solution in creative art and artist? Yes, that furrowing and hallowing of life is the element needed by our civilization now. Great art alone can prevent us from becoming spiritually paralyzed by our standardizations, from being sterilized mechanical systems, losing the rich and potent sense of life, the gift which we see here as the beauty of these little shells in their natural behavior concerning housing. When we see what is done by these forms of life on the lower plane, then we may glimpse something of what we should be doing now on our own higher plane. Unhappily, we are not doing anything so valid. Very little like it. Why are we not? Good architects are creative members of our society. The preservation of the integrity of individuality and thus making beautiful, in various characteristic ways, the common necessity: that is our job. I do not think you could have a better instance of generic principle at work as free individuality than in these little 'homes.'

PECTEN (SCALLOP)

"What conclusion? Once you understand the principle upon which this differentiation of expression—individuality—depends you may astonish your kind by your prolific imaginative capacity. To turn out a rationally different design from the one you did before will be conceivable, probably inevitable. The secret of true variety of which principle is susceptible is inherent in Nature. She is jealous of it! If an architect does not have that secret within his reach, his work will not be the work of a great architect. The key to creation will not be in him. An architect cannot tell you what life is, but he can tell you what is alive. We need better architects. Democracy cannot import them. Democracy can only grow them."

ADVENTURES IN THE DESERT

In 1925 during an enforced absence from Taliesin we stayed temporarily in Chicago, doing everything in our power to re-establish our lives so that we could work unhindered by financial difficulties. One happy morning my husband received a telegram from Albert McArthur, who had worked for him in the old Oak Park studio, asking him now to come as soon as possible to Phoenix to help with the design for the Arizona Biltmore Hotel. It was a godsend to us. We left next day for Phoenix.

There was much work, a new life, new friends, among them Dr. Alexander Chandler who owned the fashionable Hotel San Marcos in the small town of Chandler, and whose dream it was to build a new resort to be called San Marcos in the Desert. The building of the Arizona Biltmore was well on its way at the time and we moved into the San Tan Mountains near Chandler where we built a temporary camp on a site made available by Dr. Chandler. We called it "Ocatillo," after the cactus that grew abundantly all over the mountain slopes, and built fifteen cabins of wood with white canvas wings, that looked like little ships in the desert. We took long horseback rides and walks over the sharp paths made by the Indians.

The desert experience was new and exciting. We loved our white ships scattered over the hard, forbidding ground, with the self-sufficient cacti protecting themselves from intruders like us. Everything in the desert is sparse and abstract, and we studied its magnificent structural inventiveness.

"Arizona needs its own architecture," my husband later wrote. "The straight line and broad plane should come here—of all places—to become the dotted line, the textured, broken plane, for in all the vast desert there is not one hard undotted line! Arizona's long, low, sweeping lines, uptilting planes, surfaces patterned after such abstractions in line and color as find 'realism' in the patterns of the rattlesnake, the Gilamonster, the chameleon and the sahuaro, cholla, or staghorn,—or is it the other way around—are inspiration enough. But there lie her great striated and stratified masses, too, noble and quiet. And great nature masonry rising from the mesa floor is all the noble architecture she has at present. Pattern of future Arizona architecture? The sahuaro. The sahuaro itself is a perfect example of 'reinforced' construction. With its interior vertical rods it holds upright the great columnar mass for six centuries or more. A truer skyscraper than the functioneer builds.

"The desert shows a remarkable scientific building economy in these constructions. And the desert could teach any architect applying

"OCATILLO" DESERT CAMP, SALT RANGE, NEAR CHANDLER, ARIZONA

for lessons. He may see the reinforcing rod employed in the flesh of the sahuaro but he may see the lattice reed and welded tubular construction in the stalk of the cholla, the staghorn, the bignana. Even the flesh of the prickly pear is worth studying for structure. In most of the cacti she employs box to box or cellular construction. She makes it everywhere strongly effective without having to reduce the scheme to post and girder construction before she can 'figure' it out. She has this great advantage of our very best engineers."

We fell in love with the desert and decided to build a permanent camp on some suitable site. I always liked Phoenix and was able to convince my husband to buy property some twenty miles away from town. We immediately proceeded to build, at first with textiles, stone, and redwood. We had little money in those years and it was cheaper to use canvas extensively, as well as the native rock which we hauled from our own mountains. We used the redwood, the lowest priced lumber yet very appropriate and colorful, with white canvas. Steel and glass were added only later.

The buildings of our camp look as though they were excavated rather than built, and yet they are prodigiously modern. People from many parts of the world have come to see Taliesin West, walking in

TALIESIN WEST, PARADISE VALLEY, NEAR SCOTTSDALE, ARIZONA

TALIESIN WEST. LIVING ROOM

wonder through the large, sweeping planting areas and hidden gardens, fountains flowing and blending in the vast freedom of space. The sense of space permeates Taliesin West so breathtakingly that the buildings, the desert and mountains become fused, the walls vanish and at times the camp looks like a mirage in the desert appearing and disappearing in a shimmering, ethereal light. In all his buildings Frank Lloyd Wright created a "depth dimension" which no other architect achieved, the sense of spirit and form as one that marks all his works. In the Taliesin buildings, with their massive sculptural walls integral with the surrounding mountains, their angles flawless in form and proportion, there is a freshness and freedom of spirit that fills every line and plane.

He was extremely interested in supervising the details of every building he designed for others, but not for us, at Taliesin, and he would declare proudly, "You know the shoemaker's children always go without shoes." So both Taliesins were inadequately taken care of in details. I would reprimand him: "We haven't finished this wing yet and you are already working on another one."

"Anybody can do that," he would say. "Anybody can finish it—I must sketch out new ones." And we continued to add new wings, terraces, pergolas, theaters, even a restaurant.

He loved the theater at Taliesin West which he called "The Cabaret." He wanted it to be a place where people could have dinner and look at motion pictures or listen to music without disturbance and undue locomotion. For dining he designed and built simple narrow concrete projections on the back of each row of seats because he wanted it all done as quickly as possible. "Some day I will design the tables," he said. He liked to do everything with speed. Nothing should take time. Consequently the execution of details was conspicuously missing. "Taliesin West is only a sketch," he would say. "Someday you are going to finish it." And we are now finishing and perfecting it. His complete design for the development of Taliesin West will take us years to finish. We are continuing to expand, in need of more space as the Taliesin Fellowship moves ahead in work and play.

"A DESERT BUILDING SHOULD BE NOBLY SIMPLE IN OUTLINE AS THE REGION ITSELF IS SCULPTURED, SHOULD HAVE LEARNED FROM THE CACTUS MANY SECRETS OF STRAIGHT LINE PATTERN FOR ITS FORMS, PLAYING WITH THE LIGHT AND SOFTENING THE BUILDING INTO ITS PROPER PLACE AMONG THE ORGANIC DESERT CREATIONS—THE MAN-MADE BUILDING HEIGHTENING THE BEAUTY OF THE DESERT. . . ."—F.LL.W. TALIESIN WEST.

Life with him was a constantly exciting adventure. There were no stagnant periods at any time. I remember on one of our trips from Wisconsin to Arizona, when the whole Fellowship travelled in a caravan of cars, he heard of a magnificent view of the Grand Canyon from the north side rarely seen by the usual tourist. The road, however, was nearly impassable, full of "dead man's gulches," and at times there was no road at all. Without giving the adventure so much as a second thought we started over the "road" which soon disappeared altogether; we pioneered our own trail over the desert ground. There were flat tires, complaints, even hysterics. One possessive young woman who insisted on driving her own over-sized LaSalle became hysterical with exhaustion, and stopping in the middle of a desert wash, rushed over to our car screaming, "This can't go on any more! It can't! It's cruel! We'll never get there. Look what's ahead of us, mountains and stones and those horrid gulches! There aren't any roads around here! I can't!" she screamed.

"Let someone else drive your car for you. You are foolish about your car. I told you that at the beginning. Don't be so over-possessive. You are tired out from driving, that is all," I said. "If I can take it you can," and I managed to calm her down.

Soon there appeared in that wilderness the silhouette of a house; we approached it with hope. It turned out to be a little clapboard cabin post office to which people came from seventy-five miles around to get their mail. The childless old couple who lived there told us that our destination, a place called Tuweep, had no water and that another fifty miles of unknown desert lay ahead of us. It was then that my own spirit began to weaken, and I asked to go back, but no matter how reasonably I pleaded, my husband was relentless. His eyes were brilliant with challenge. "Never you mind," he said, "get back into the cars. We're going on!" When he turned to speak to the man and wife, they warned: "Save your water, mister. There isn't any to be had after you leave here. And we don't want to have to send out a search party for you."

We started out again, bumping over the wretched road for several hours, until we arrived at the mythical outpost of Tuweep at night. It was nine o'clock. Except for the lights of the car, we were in solid darkness, and we somehow gathered dry wood, sparse as it was, and built a big fire. My husband solemnly reminded us, "Remember, every drop of water is valuable—waste none—and keep the fires going all night because there are mountain lions in this neck of the woods." Some of the more sophisticated tried to laugh, but then everyone fell silent and began his assigned work. Later we huddled by the fire which warmed our spirits as well as our exhausted bodies.

Our work was based, then as now, on the rotation system and that night a fiery young blonde woman was on duty to look after the supper. We had roasted wieners served on paper plates, some milk, crackers and cookies. One of the boys complained to the young woman: "Why didn't you bring the mustard along? Imagine eating wieners without mustard!" Her straight figure outlined by firelight, the wind occasionally scattering sparks, her gold hair flying wildly in every direction, she turned on him in fury: "Here we are, surrounded by mountain lions, stranded, we don't even know if we'll ever survive or get back to civilization, we hardly have any water left and all *you* can think about is *mustard!* If you die first, I'll write 'I only wanted mustard' on your tombstone."

My husband then asked a Polish student, Marya Lilien, to sing a few of her national songs: "Something optimistic—just for reassurance," he said. As she sang for us we gradually all joined in, circled close around the fire, gladly inhaling the clean cold air of the desert night. The darkness deepened and people threw down their sleeping bags in various places near the circle of firelight.

At sunrise Mr. Wright was up first. I was still asleep. "Olgivanna," I heard him call. "Get up and look!" I leaped out of my sleeping bag, throwing a blanket over my shoulders, and as I stood beside him I saw to my horror that we had laid our sleeping bags no more than four feet from a sheer drop-off of the Grand Canyon. If we had driven our cars a few yards further . . . A terrible thought. We had been so tired the night before that we had done no exploring, and did not notice a precipice that plunged more than one mile down into the Colorado River. We looked cautiously over the edge. Far beneath us the river wound like a thin gray snake. We quietly put on our warm, heavy clothes and sat down by the blazing breakfast fire. The sun was rising now above those prehistoric rock-hewn plateaus and the colors unfolded over the canyon in fantastic beauty. "After all," my husband said, "this is what we came for. And it was all worth it."

THE LIVING CITY

I do not like cities," he said. "I think the city did its work long ago. The city now is a habit; we do not need it; it is in the way and we could get along very well without it if we were sufficiently intelligent. The more intelligent people are continually leaving it and those who have not had the experience crowd in where they have been.

"What we need is the wedding of the city and the country. I designed Broadacre City on that idea and modeled it in 1933. There you have all the advantages of the city, without the city. And the country is not spoiled, because quality in building comes into the picture to save it from destruction. You can build an organic house anywhere and it will not spoil anything; so you could build an organic city out in the country and not hurt the country. But you cannot take the country into the city; the city has to go to the country. It certainly is proceeding now. It is nothing that I have invented. The little gas station was the first sign, then the produce markets and the merchants going out. The best people are already gone and the city is a kind of gregarious hangover at the present time.

"There is no room for architecture in the city. The car destroyed it; the telephone, telegraph, television, radio, all destroyed it because they are just as available in the country as in town. There is no advan-

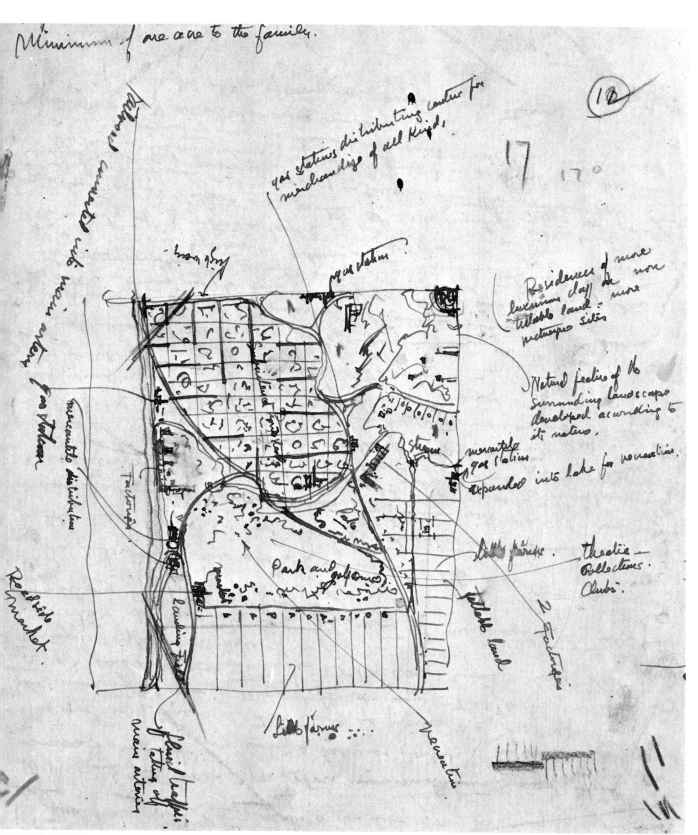

Minimum of one acre to the family.

gas station distributing center for merchandise of all kind.

gas station

17 17°

Residences of more luxurious class on non tillable land - more picturesque sites

Natural feature of the surrounding landscape developed according to its nature.

mercantile gas station

expanded into lake for recreation.

little farms.

theatre Collections Clubs.

Park and golf course

tillable land

2 Factories

Little farms

little farms

recreation

ORIGINAL SKETCH FOR BROADACRE CITY

tage in the town anymore for anything. The city is going, going, gone.

"The greatest contribution I have made to architecture, I think, would be the fact that I have really subscribed to architecture, not just building, not just fashion. And I am the author—if you want to say so—of a natural architecture."

At ease and utterly free in his relationships with all people, he had no trace of snobbishness anywhere in his makeup and would speak with genuine respect to masons, carpenters and porters, and with as much consideration for them as for the President of the United States. It was that natural sense of equality, an indigenous freedom and grace, that his architecture expressed. He exalted the man working in a factory and the woman sitting all day at an office desk. Though they might have to work there with back aching and eyes tired, in a building of beauty they could look up and be refreshed and inspired to continue their work. There is a great principle in this, so simple that it is often overlooked. Because his ideals were not unreal abstractions and the ideal of democracy was deep within him, at the foundation of his being, his buildings are not abstract concepts detached from man's needs. Always living organisms representing man, they present the best in him, whether in a modest house or a large structure. Everything Frank Lloyd Wright did expressed that characteristic simplicity.

He believed the role of an architect to be that of a builder, not only of buildings but of the social structure, because he felt that if society were given conditions in which buildings had intelligence and *raison d'être* the whole structure of human society itself would have the substance of strength and beauty. Interested in politics and affairs of state, he believed that architecture as the plan-in-structure of all things was the all-inclusive basis for every civilization and culture. So he repeatedly related architecture to democracy, considering democracy the highest form of aristocracy man has ever known, a society based on the sovereignty of the individual; the truly noble building therefore was an aristocratic building.

He sometimes connected his architecture with Christ's doctrine, which he felt was misunderstood by ascetics who denied the world and therefore the earth which he loved. Because he was constantly in the process of changing and growing, he created a limitless variety of buildings, all based on the same principle and all as different in expression as were the people and surroundings for which they were designed. One can always recognize his works, though they often no more resemble one another than Paris resembles New York, because they are all characterized by knowledge of principle and faith in man. He felt that it was the lack of these that must result in the kind of dead building of which we now have so many, everywhere, especially in the Americas. The "Internationalist" boxes, big and little, square, rectangular and round, have spread throughout Europe as well. Of course Frank Lloyd Wright's influence could have been greater, but it was enough to prevent a total influx of such sterile structures which glorify the mechanics of expedient building and ignore the human spirit, modern buildings which are mainly lifeless machines, push-button buildings which create push-button people who hardly look alive as they work, so affected are they by their surroundings.

It is still too easy to build buildings without intelligence in them, to take the path of least resistance, to erect a brittle skyscraper made of glass, divided by little steel partitions. The making of an individual design requires humane thought and experience, of which so little seems to be left now in our life harassed by the expedient everywhere. In such an environment, the sense of architecture in its essential function as an organic part of society is still largely missing from our life. It is this that Frank Lloyd Wright fought against in a constant effort to protect his country from architects without faith in the individual, who disregard man as man, and whose buildings nullify him into anonymity. He abhorred the confusion and congestion of modern big cities, predicting that they would perish. It now seems that his prophecy is being fulfilled. He had foreseen clearly the dreadful loss of energy, the draining tenacity required of the human body to endure the noise, the crashing of wheels and metal, the heavy fumes and smog of our gasoline-saturated cities. But he knew that man's heroism would keep him living and producing in order to make a more civilized future.

He designed Broadacre City as a rejection of the present-day city. Free, self-sufficient, with its own forests, gardens and agriculture, this Living City—as he later called it—is designed to replace the stifling, disorderly, strangling city of today. He describes it: "The model of Broadacre City is an attack upon the cultural lag of our society," he wrote. "The model attempts to show how a more humane use of our vast

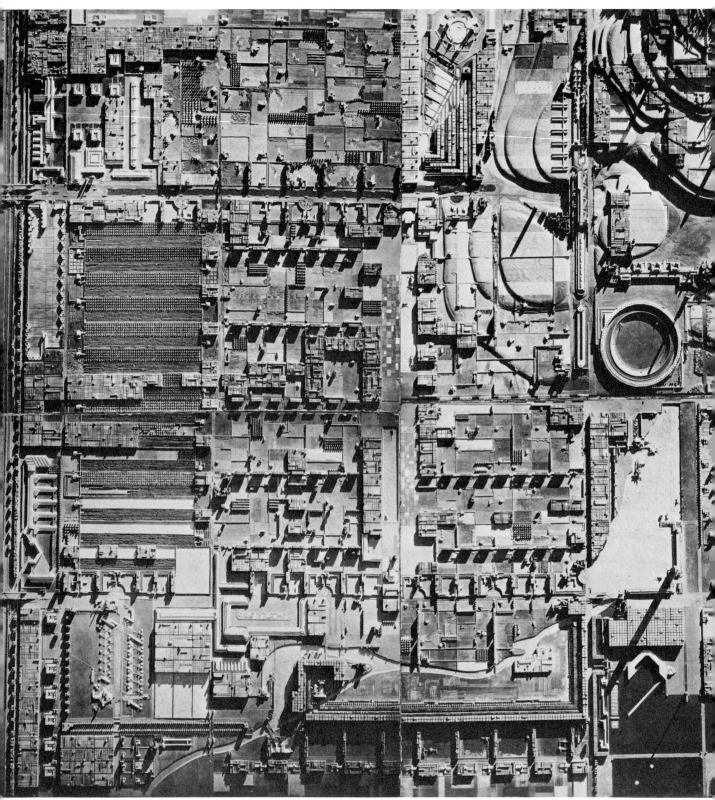

BROADACRE CITY. MODEL

machine leverage could *free* the citizens; and that freedom could be accomplished by way of his own architecture. To that end, were the machine put in its proper place now, its place would be in the hand of the creative architect. Or let us better say, architecture creative. *Democracy can arrive no other way.* We should then soon realize that the right buildings for the right people in the right places, if building were more organic, would naturally form a harmonious relationship. Each building, though all differed totally, would be naturally complementary to the others. Were that to happen I see no reason why habituated city dwellers, now living on a perch, could not come into direct association with those who live on the ground and for the ground, until they too would themselves have learned to love the ground for itself. The individual home on its acre (or more) together with the utility buildings of everyday American life all form a harmonious whole. If all were now to be built according to nature (either human nature or the nature of outdoors) this is not an unreasonable supposition. That organic harmony is what I have aimed at here.

"I should say the only place for a skyscraper is in the country in its own park. There habituated urbanites might have direct association with country life and agrarian ideals, while their children grew up under conditions more favorable to their future as human beings. All artificial distinctions between city, suburb and country are modified or abolished. The model shows how to end the useless back and forth haul and the senseless human travel to and fro of our present wasteful and wasting traffic situation. Waste of time and life is in Broadacre City everywhere lessened or ended altogether in favor of a better use of life, a fresh opportunity to understand ourselves, and time to cultivate leisure in enjoyment of our own better nature. The machine could give us this modern opportunity if we used it properly. That more appropriate use of power must be the aim of our culture if our civilization is ever to reach the state of organic democracy. There is no other democracy.

"Suppose we call organic architecture a *natural* architecture for a natural life—building for and with the individual as distinguished from the pseudo-classic order of our American schools mainly derived today from survivals of moribund military and monarchic orders; and distinguished from that later attempt at elimination of individuality—the journalistic classification grafted upon organic architecture, called by ambitious provincials the 'International Style'; distinguished from any preconceived formula whatever for mere appearances.

"Yes, we might say organic architecture is *informal* architecture—symmetry within rather than obvious. Architecture in the reflex? Architecture seeking to *serve* man rather than to become those forces now trying so hard to rule over him. Here then is good reason to say organic architecture is the natural architecture of a democracy, instead of various Fascist hangovers from earlier continental cultures.

"Organic architecture is the expression of innate character. Can there then be question of the many, or any, 'styles'? No, but essential Style must be in all buildings, provided only that it is understood and naturally achieved from within the nature of the building itself. True style is always found within the very means which build the building, because character is the secret of style and is the expression of principle at work from within. In this *interior* sense then, let us say that Broadacre City is the free city of democracy and as such would inevitably arrive at style of its own. The great free city of democracy will have style all its own; style then becomes something more spontaneous and natural than the academies have yet dared preach. Nothing in the free city need be merely something exterior, therefore, forced. Force can organize nothing—either in its own structure or imposed upon its people by Classic, that is to say *exterior*, discipline. The people of such a city as Broadacre City could never be ruled by authoritarian classification or suffer dictatorial establishment. Architecture and agrarian acreage will be seen together with landscape, as landscape. The best native architectures of the world have been and still are great architectures which arose within the lifetime of the civilizations they actually served to express. Academic architecture always belied or bedeviled this natural architecture, throughout Europe especially.

"If we, as a people, were ever to understand the principles of organic architecture, which are the same as those of our own spiritual human nature, a basic change would be necessary in our way of education. And if we were to learn to use our machines and vast stores of material according to a faithful sense of their fitness to humane purpose, we should inevitably, I believe, arrive not only at new forms of building but a greatly expanded life that had a true style of our own. Perhaps, too, our nation would arrive at what, if looked back upon in distance of time, might be seen as the free Usonian style of the twentieth century. But should that ever occur it could not come by calculated intention. It

THE PRICE TOWER, H. C. PRICE CO., BARTLESVILLE, OKLAHOMA

would come by honest production and long-continued experiment on our part as *individuals*. Style is a desirable circumstance always because style is character. But 'a style' is, always, the death of style.

"Because we are chiefly concerned with the integrity of structure that we call organic architecture, where we first grasped the spiritual sense of this modern demand for a new and higher order of things than was imagined or accepted by authoritarian cultures as 'classic,' I have come to believe that only the mind imbued with such deeper sense of *structure* can perceive this fine integrity as a fundamental social necessity. Democracy demands and must create more livable and gracious human simplicities, perceiving anew those simples which were ever the necessity to a good life; but not so to such academic substitutes-for-culture as now bear the authorized hallmark of these United States. War would be unthinkable to the people of a Broadacre City. The black and white of bipartisanship would give way to more color: three parties, at least, and the minority report more interesting to them all.

"Now while these new, swollen material means of today, of which we boast, dam the life-blood and emasculate the manhood of this nation, we must think of all this and keep on thinking. But if the same mechanical means now abused by us were used with more intelligent self-interest to increase the spaciousness, graciousness and happiness of human living here on earth; if we were intelligently to back up the enlarged sense and appropriate uses of space that are good for organic architecture, mechanizing, so used, would automatically enable this free

BROADACRE CITY, MODEL OF TYPICAL HOME FOR SLOPING GROUND

city of modern life to be realized. By appropriate use of the new *space-scale* of organic architecture—if the human being were used as a time-scale you would see the extended highway as the horizontal line of Usonian freedom expanding by mobilization everywhere. You will then see something of the modern Usonian freedom expanding by mobilization everywhere. You will then see something of the modern Usonian city that is approaching you in Broadacres.

"You may see the design of the modern farm itself, little or big, in its true relation to adjoining buildings. You see the sizes and shapes of dwelling plots, parks and fields, all laid out in good proportion each to each and each one to all. You see the whole man-built occupation of

BROADACRE CITY. MODEL, CIVIC CENTER AT THE COUNTY SEAT SHOWING OFFICES ACROSS THE SMALL LAKE. SMALL INDUSTRIES AND APARTMENTS IN BACKGROUND.

the land adapted to natural contours with forestation, and tillage becoming a charming feature of landscape; hedgeways, ravines and waterways themselves becoming boundaries. All this together is completely rhythmic in relation to good, well-considered buildings, well related to each other on well-placed roads. You see 'horizontal farming,' contour-plowing, properly applied to crops, pastures, animals—all well related to the people. And when you see these varied, multi-various parts all contributing to a great dramatic whole, you sense the repose of contentment and exuberance of plenty—yes, and aesthetic, truly, in the over-all view. You are getting a glimpse of the organic character of life in a modern city, agrarian-loving, such as here planned: the organic Usonian city of our future, if we have any future as a democracy. Were we to use our material means to such ends, we might then boast of the *culture* of our nation and justify our civilization. Our forefathers had some right, and good reason, too, to expect such culture of the republic they were then pleased to prophesy as democratic. Their prophecy is still our hope!"

Frank Lloyd Wright's vision of the city will prevail when the principle on which he designed the Mile-High Building takes hold, a magnificent idea which would sweep clean all the debris of our cities. In this concept, cities would be composed of a few mile-high buildings set among acres of forested ground and blossoming gardens. The problem of thousands of people trafficking to their offices at the same hour is taken care of by soaringly beautiful towers, with elevators which move like trains from floor to floor, opening their doors at several floors simultaneously, and with adequate parking facilities and shops all contained within each building standing free in its own wide green park.

If our cities are not changed by the conscious will of the people, they will be forced to change automatically. It is a necessary, unavoidable, revolutionary change in a time when there can be no more piling up of one glass skyscraper on top of another, an architecture for robots.

But no matter how huge or ill-planned our cities are, they cannot uproot the idea of democracy as natural to the human organism, the greatest idea for a society of man yet revealed by history. Finding a true expression in the United States, this idea cannot perish though

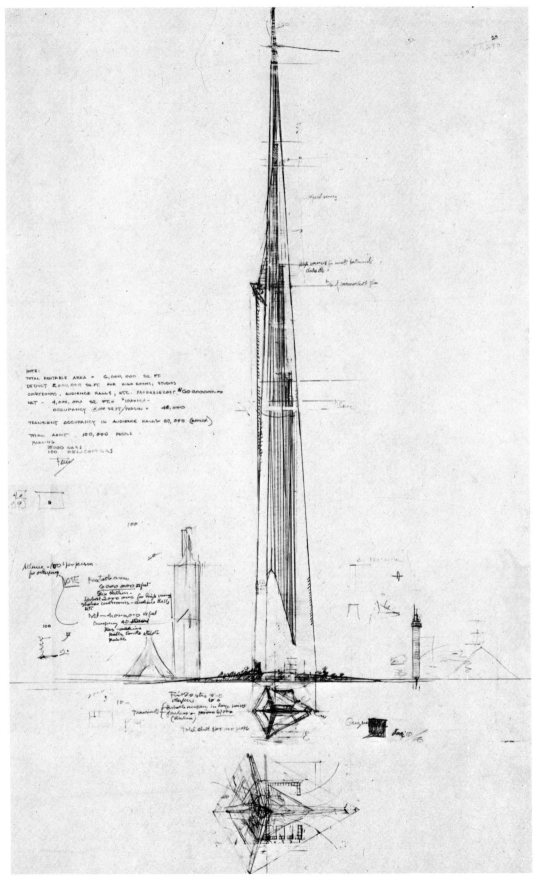

ORIGINAL SKETCH FOR "THE MILE-HIGH"

the city itself may perish. The idea of democracy will eventually forge a world in which man is proud to live, a world whose attainment depends upon the American youth sufficiently dissatisfied with the disorderliness of the life and architecture around him to seek a way out by expanding the basic principle of organic architecture. They will be young men and women willing to render quality in whatever they do, willing not to rush quickly after fame and riches, willing to wait, to put material ambition second to the wealth of their inner life. This needs of course a waiting based on strength, not on laziness or passivity. In buildings based on the principle of organic architecture, man will once more recognize himself as human and will create the future America was formed to realize.

In this light, the thesis of organic architecture is simple: the basic idea that an organic building is designed appropriately for the people who will live or work in it, for its site, for its purpose, for the geographic, climatic and economic conditions in which it is to exist. As such, the nature of the design must be *individual*, whether it is a house or a church, a bank or business building or department store. It will not have a pleasing appearance merely from one side, with another side which does not spell out a harmonious architectural grammar. It will be well-coordinated in all its aspects, taking shape from its inner reality—an entity.

This is the principle of organic architecture we teach and practice in our work in Wisconsin and in Arizona. Every building that leaves our drafting room has in it the labor of love to give it its individual entity, no matter how humble or grand the structure may be.

The power of an idea is imparted forever if those individuals close, either physically or spiritually, to its originator, have the necessary understanding of it. They must struggle in order to actualize it, but eventually the idea will triumph. We at Taliesin are the heirs to the tradition of Frank Lloyd Wright. He used to tell our young people:

"You must be in love with architecture. Forget it as a profession. It will soon come your way in that sense. But be in love with it. Architecture is a dedication to something holy, to which I render my service. And so you will be what you wish to be. You will be successful in the right way. Your success will come—not by vanity, not by way of ambition, but naturally—the way it came to me naturally, although I waited almost sixty years. I hope you live as long as I have lived."

He was the first to see the possibilities of the machine used, not as an end in itself, but as a tool to serve man. In 1894 he wrote his famous Hull House lecture on "The Art and Craft of the Machine," which has since gone around the world. And fifty years later, he gave a talk to our students on the same subject:

"If you have the thing deep enough and the love is there—if you are enamored, if you make the sacrifices—you will become an architect. You must want to be one more than anything else in the world. You must love it for something within yourself that is bigger than you are, and you must be willing to pay the price of becoming what you want to be. Nobody knows what that price is going to be.

"I don't know how many of you are making real sacrifices to become an architect. It would be rather fruitless to ask the question, how many of you are throwing in everything that you ever had or hoped to have, regardless, to become an architect. Some of you are. I think most of you would.

"I think if you deliberately are careless about making any mistake and think it is not important and do not put your best effort into it, believing it with all your might to be right, the mistake is not going to do you any good. It is only when you believe with the strength of your whole nature that it is right and then find out that you are mistaken that you learn. Then you begin to add tired to tired and add it again. So by way of your mistakes you develop, you grow. But only if they are an agony to you and if they go deep enough into your consciousness so that you know why they were mistakes—the next time you will not make them.

"The artist must have a single purpose, singlemindedness, and ability to stick to the centerline of what he really is, what he loves. If he loves enough, he will gain enough. And of course loves manifests itself according to your own nature. One man will show it in one way and another man in another way, but if it is not there, there is not much use wasting time either for him or for us. The best thing for him to do is to knock around loose until he hits something. Usually it will be something that hits him. And wakes him up.

"An artist needs to pay attention to his inner vision. That is what makes him an artist and differentiates him from most other men who try to carve out a career or gratify an instinct. The artist must listen to an inner voice and he must have conviction and he must cultivate all resources in him that contribute to his vision.

"Now what distinguishes an artist from a scientist? What qualities are in his nature? The scientist has curiosity; he takes things apart and investigates; he tries to put them together again and soldom succeeds, but he is a great hand at taking things apart. Now, the artist as distinguished from the scientist—what is his quality of nature? He sees things together. He sees not only the separate units going in this or that direction, but also the concordance of the whole. Given that quality of mind that looks at things that way, you soon develop an overall vision. That vision goes further and embraces more than this particularity of vision which is scientific, or business, or materialistic. Truly it is what you call spiritual. It is of the spirit of the man, informing and pushing and developing him into something uncommon, unusual, because the altogether is extremely unusual. To see things as a whole is not what most human beings do. And so far as we know education now, it seeks to *condition* the man instead of *enlighten* him. By endeavoring to teach an artist, you may condition him; you are unlikely to enlighten him because it is very difficult to enable him by way of what you can teach him to grasp this sense of the whole, this oneness, this coming together and each taking its place where it belongs in the great scheme of things. That is what you want to pay attention to in yourselves. When you see something that interests you, when you are up against a circumstance either in nature or in your own experience and it puzzles you and you don't understand, try to see it in relation to the whole. Dr. Einstein was perfectly right in his doctrine of relativity. Nothing has any real consequence in itself. It is only as it is related to other things and in that relationship do you find what is interesting to an architect, an architect being inevitably a builder. He coordinates, he is a concatenator, and of course he is a relentless observer. A natural architect never misses anything out of the corner of his eye; he sees what is going on, not so much in itself, but in relation to a sense of the whole. Of course that is what is missing in education. There, you go for one thing, then you go for something else, then for another. And you can't call it training. That is the difficulty. You cannot train this gathering in to the whole. You can admonish; you can be an exemplar; you can do it and be it yourself and young people around you may grasp it or they may not. When you are all here together as you are, there should be an inner urge, a great depth of desire to be creative as an architect, as a human

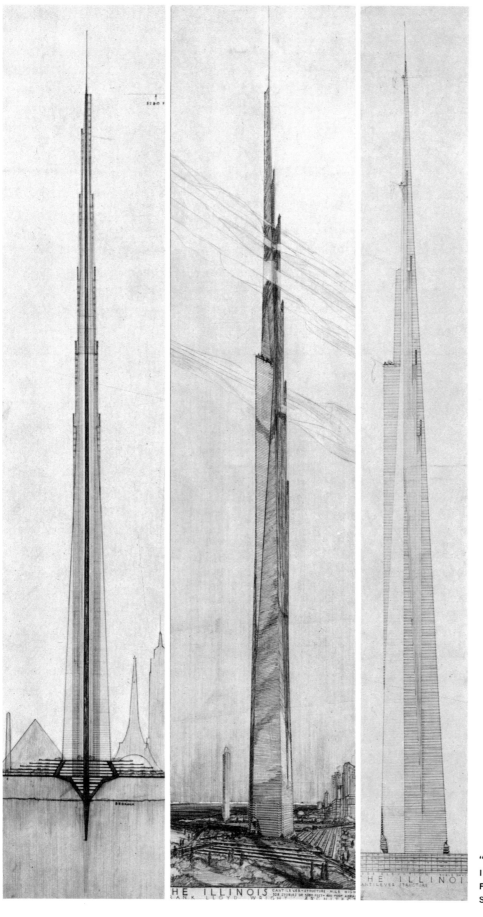

"THE MILE-HIGH," CHICAGO, ILLINOIS: LEFT, TAPROOT FOUNDATION; CENTER, PERSPECTIVE; RIGHT, ELEVATION.

being, and a ceaseless vigilance concerning everything you observe as to its meaning, its significance, its true place; and there gradually takes place in your mind a sense of order. Not just physical order, but a sense of the great order—a becoming never finished. Only as you perceive it as a principle working in all you do are you beginning to be awake. That is why probably 99 people out of 100 are what might be called asleep. They have not awakened to the magnificent inspiration of this sense of the whole. That is what is needed in architecture now and that is why architecture has been moribund for 500 years, at least since the Renaissance, but it was dead before that. There has been no great new life of the spirit coming into architecture since the Gothic cathedrals and there was not too much then. But there was something.

"And now we are off again on the right foot because of steel, glass, concrete, all the new materials that we have; the machine, the old lever which was originally the wheel, the original lever, with which they built the pyramids. Now we have a leverage that is applicable to nearly everything we do. That leverage is the machine. This new element in architecture which we call tenuity, that was never possible until this century. That has changed the whole fabric and substance of architecture—just that one circumstance. Added to that is the mechanical proficiency in being able indefinitely to stamp out a thing. For a million years you could go on repeating and make it as complicated almost as you please. The whole basis of building a building, or the act of building, has changed. How important it is, therefore, that today we cultivate and cherish this sense of the whole; it is the only thing now that can bring us out of this chaos in which we are—and God knows you can see it when you go into any city in the United States or in Europe for that matter. In the Middle Ages cities were entities. They existed because of the good spiritual life in them. But now they are dead. They do not exist in that sense anymore. Something else is taking place. What is it that is taking place? What is it now that can be done to bring life again into accord in a beautiful whole? There is nothing that can be done except as the architect does it. It is suddenly possible—and it *is* suddenly because it is only since about 1893 that this ever became evident as an idea, the idea of organic architecture."

FALLINGWATER

In 1933, Edgar Kaufmann, Jr., a young man who had an unusual understanding and appreciation of Mr. Wright's work, became a member of the Taliesin Fellowship. Shortly thereafter when his father and mother were planning to build a house at Bear Run near Pittsburgh, Edgar prevailed upon them to have Mr. Wright design it.

They came to Taliesin and explained what they wanted in the way of a house, but little did they dream that their house, which Mr. Wright named "Fallingwater," would become famous throughout the world.

In 1938, two years after the house was built, my husband wrote in the *Architectural Forum*: "This building is a late example of the inspiration of a site, the cooperation of an intelligent, appreciative client, and the use of entirely masonry materials except for an interlining of redwood and asphalt beneath all flooring. Again, by way of steel in tension, this building takes its place and achieves its form. . . . This structure might serve to indicate that the sense of shelter—the sense of space where used with sound structural sense—has no limitations as to form except the materials used and the methods by which they are employed for what purpose. The ideas involved here are in no wise changed from those of early work. The materials and methods of construction come through them, here, as they may and will come through everywhere.

KAUFMANN HOUSE, "FALLINGWATER," BEAR RUN, PENNSYLVANIA

That is all. The effects you see in this house are not superficial effects."

When he was asked many years later how he related the site to the house, Mr. Wright replied: "There in a beautiful forest was a solid high rock-ledge rising beside a waterfall and the natural thing seemed to be to cantilever the house from that rock-bank over the falling water. You see, in the Bear Run house, the first house where I came into possession of concrete and steel with which to build, of course the grammar of that house cleared up on that basis. Then came (of course) Mr. Kaufmann's love for the beautiful site. He loved the site where the house was built and liked to listen to the waterfall. So that was a prime motive in the design. I think you can hear the waterfall when you look at the design. At least it is there and he lives intimately with the thing he loves."

The construction of this house formed the basis of a lifelong friendship with Mr. and Mrs. Kaufmann and Edgar Kaufmann, Jr. Whenever my husband and I went to visit them through the years it was always a new experience to come under the magic of the soaring flight of imagination, the exquisite poetry, embodied in Fallingwater.

I remember my husband coming back to the room where we were staying, just after talking with Mr. Kaufmann, Sr., who was not well at the time, and saying: "Well, Olgivanna, I just heard a very nice thing from E. J. [as he called him]. He was sitting up in bed, gazing at me with a serious look in his eyes and he said: 'Frank Lloyd Wright, I have spent much money in my life but I never got anything so worthwhile for it as this house. Thank you.'"

In 1963, Edgar Kaufmann, Jr. gave the house in trust for public use to the Western Pennsylvania Conservancy and provided the funds as well for its maintenance; fortunately the house would be preserved without change.

KAUFMANN HOUSE

"IDEAS CAME TUMBLING UP
AND OUT ONTO PAPER"

1936 was a lean year for Taliesin. We had felt the effects of the depression that gripped the country and though our work and expenses went on, architectural commissions were very few. At that difficult time we had a visit from Herbert Johnson, the head of the Johnson Wax company. They needed an administration building to house their expanding organization.

Frank Lloyd Wright attacked this new project with the greed of a man starved for work. "What a release of pent-up energy—the making of those plans," he wrote. "Ideas came tumbling up and out onto paper. . . ." He worked days and nights on the design of the building. He then made, by his own count, 132 trips by car from Taliesin to Racine to superintend the structure over a period of two years. He was fortunate to have as contractor Ben Wiltscheck whom he was deeply fond of, and the Taliesin Fellowship, mainly Wesley Peters and Edgar Tafel, to supervise construction.

One of the most beautiful features of the design consisted of graceful, slender columns only nine inches in diameter at the foot, which stood as if on tiptoe and soared up twenty-four feet high, spreading at the top like lily pads to become the ceiling. According to the building code regulations each of the concrete columns would have to be three feet in diameter, instead of nine inches, to carry its necessary load of twelve tons.

Mr. Wright and Mr. Johnson asked the building commission for permission to make a test. In their confidence of success they had already made the steel forms. An exact duplicate of the column was placed on the site and anybody who wanted to come that day was welcome. The field was crowded, the commissioners, newspapermen, the townspeople, all irresistibly drawn to the scene, and a steam shovel began dumping bags of gravel and cement on top of the slender stem. Mr. Wright watched, with a woolen shawl on his shoulders, while the crane swung through the cold air and flung so many cement bags as to form a mountain; all day until the sun went down, the bags were

THE TEST COLUMN

thrown, the mountain kept growing. As the crowd kept gathering, the police, dreading the collapse of the column, roped off the area. But the column stood there, powerful in its slenderness because the architect had given it a circular membrane of steel which had become one with the flesh of concrete. By the end of the day, the brave shaft was carrying sixty tons, instead of the twelve tons that were supposed to break it. There was no more room at the top. Mr. Wright gave the word to break it. It was finally pushed over, the crash of cement shook the streets around, but the column, now lying on the ground, was still unbroken. Only the head had come off. The commissioner vanished in silence.

Those tapering columns now support a building recognized as one of the most beautiful and efficient in the world; the story has been carried everywhere by the press, on radio, television and the movies.

And years later, in 1948-1949, the administration building was joined by a research tower, also designed by Mr. Wright. It stands there nearby with light grace, familiar to Americans and to people all over the world who visit the Johnson buildings in crowds as they do a historic monument—a mark of American culture.

S. C. JOHNSON AND SON, INC. RESEARCH TOWER, RACINE, WISCONS

ON THE ARTS

Early in our life together we discovered that he and I had had the same dream in our youths. Mine began when I was only fourteen and I first heard the great artist Huberman play the violin. The hall he played in was ugly, with glaring, distracting lights and poor acoustics; the people were noisy, gesticulating with their programs and whispering. With eyes closed I sat there dreaming that I would some day have a beautiful theatre of my own, with a quiet intimate atmosphere and I would be able to listen to music without having to isolate myself from crinkling papers and chattering tongues.

When we met I told that to Mr. Wright. "Well, Olgivanna," he said. "I've had exactly the same dream. But what I said to myself was, 'Someday I am going to build a theatre and it will be my theatre. I will hear great artists, I will have superb productions and my own chamber orchestra to play in an intimate environment I will create myself.'" We were both sure then that this was symbolic.

As I have told, the first thing we did when we revived the old Hillside School in Wisconsin was to transform the gymnasium into a theatre, the first theatre of our own, and we created it together. At the beginning of the Fellowship we showed only moving pictures there. Then we invited professors, writers, ministers, rabbis, many fine speakers who delivered their talks from our small stage, and later we gave plays and skits of our own. In time we enlarged the theatre, and in Taliesin West in Arizona we built the Pavilion, in which performances are given by our chamber music orchestra and a cappella choir; and the annual Music and Dance Festival has become an established Taliesin tradition, which people from all over the country have come to see.

My husband would listen insatiably to music for hours at a time. Loud-speakers, concealed in various places around Taliesin, played for five or six hours during the day, until everybody begged me to have them turned off. To him a building too sang: architecture was a harmony of planes, depths and heights, the spirit of life, "the expression of man," and so he spoke in terms of the structural quality of a musical composition. He believed that, in an inner sense, music and architecture are one. Whenever he heard a symphony orchestra or our chamber music ensemble he was hardly aware of the musicians, listening directly to the work of the composer, so that when some famous cellist or violinist came to Taliesin to play for us I sometimes had to nudge him to remind him that the performer needed praise also. But he would insist, "It is the composer who is the creator of the music."

"But there would be no music if we had no musicians to play it," I argued. "What good is a fine composition played by a poor musician? He has to be a creative interpreter."

"That is secondary," he answered. "It is the composer we should consider first."

His favorite among all composers was Beethoven, the cause of frequent disagreement between us. I insisted that Bach was Beethoven's equal. "No, I don't believe that Bach is the equal of Beethoven. I think he is fine, but Beethoven surpasses him in creative force." He never tired of listening to his music. Through all the rooms and corridors, hills and meadows of Taliesin, there reverberated the symphonies and sonatas of Beethoven.

But for the exception of George Gershwin, who he said was a creative artist, he wavered about jazz according to his state of mind at the moment. He frequently felt that the cacophony came from primitive tribes and had no place in our civilization. I remember on one of the Fellowship's trips to Superstition Mountain in the Arizona desert, a student had turned the radio on and suddenly we heard loud jazz as we were walking up the mountain. "Turn that off," he said. "It sounds vile in this atmosphere. Let's get away from the cesspool." And modern ballroom dancing was to him a nervous, sensuous expression which had no beauty.

He felt that modern composers were groping, fugitives from great music; none could stand up to the classical composers. He never fully accepted the modernists and often we fought, even over Debussy. Once, when listening to a composition by Hindemith, he remarked, "How terrible it is to make that man suffer with sounds and rhythms he does not understand. Those cacophonies have him like a dog by the tail. There is no modern composer who can touch Beethoven."

Besides Bach, Mozart and Vivaldi, he appreciated Chopin and Brahms, but relegated them to a secondary place; and he liked Strauss's *Ein Heldenleben*, which he associated with his own life. He also liked Wagner to some extent, but in the end was bored by him. He fought with many of his friends over Wagner's music because Wagner seemed to him to move from one problem to another without really resolving them.

As for opera, he felt that it was an outmoded form removed from living experience, that it had, in fact, become ridiculous to hear a heroine screaming, "I am dying! I am dying!" in high C. He preferred the choral music of Palestrina, even the songs of Stephen Foster and the songs of the West. To him no instrument compared to the quality of the human voice; and he loved to listen to the choir we had formed at Taliesin.

Before the founding of the Fellowship, when the children were small, we often visited his sister Jane Porter at "Tan-y-deri," a house he built in 1907 on a hill across from Taliesin. After dinner Jane would sit at the piano while he and I and the children gathered around the piano near the large stone fireplace, singing American folksongs. His baritone voice was pleasing to listen to, perfect in pitch. We felt the beauty of a strong family tie, archaic in nature, dating back to his Welsh and my Montenegrin ancestry. Every year at Christmas we gathered to sing carols and after the founding of the Fellowship the young people joined us in the living room; there were times when the unrestrained resonance of a hundred voices, including those of our guests, flooded the house. Singing carols on Christmas Day became a Taliesin tradition, which we still uphold as religiously as we did in the past.

My husband loved to improvise on the piano, often saying that he did it for me, that the source of his inspiration was our love. He liked to play in our living room in the late afternoons, sometimes in the evenings, while I sat listening, and when he finished I would walk over to the piano, place my hands on his shoulders, and say to him: "Please play some more. Your improvisation is lovely." He was so pleased when I liked it and encouraged him to improvise; sometimes he would play in a state almost approaching rapture. We have some of his improvisations recorded but the moment he knew the machine was set to record he became self-conscious and restrained; what he did spontaneously was always the best.

The setting and presentation of music were naturally very important to him and when our chamber orchestra, composed of Taliesin students, began to play in our theatre and our living room, he designed a beautiful music stand made of soft light wood cut into geometric facets, with a roof-like top which conceals the lights and holds a space in the center for flower arrangements. The performers like it because the music stays on it securely and is perfectly lit; artists who come to play for us always admire and covet the graceful music stand. Separate stands, also in wood of the same design, are grouped around for chamber ensembles.

When Mr. Wright was present, the musicians were placed to sit in the best relationship to one another, and every now and then during a concert he would lean over to one of our guests: "You see," he would whisper loudly, "our music is as good for the eye as it is for the ear. When music is visually gratifying, it acquires another dimension."

Although he loved painting and sculpture, he frequently criticized painting as an "inferior" form, essentially imitative and entirely subordinate to architecture, and he frequently referred to LeCorbusier as "the painter," not "the architect." "He should have stuck to his two-dimensional painting," he said, "instead of meddling with architecture." For the mechanical buildings in the so-called "International Style" which exerted a wide influence on young architects, he had no praise. To him the glass box raised up on posts, an easy-to-build expedient without warmth or individuality, meant the destruction of architecture.

He believed in abstract painting, which could be integrated into architecture. Yet his nature was full of paradox: he bought paintings almost wherever he went, and I would tease him about it. I remember once he brought home a painting of a tree and a house on a green hill, thoroughly representational. "Don't you think these are nice colors?" he said, a little sheepishly.

"Goodness," I exclaimed, "that is what you don't believe in and there you go buying it!"

"Well, it is all right though, rather nice. See how simply he handled the tree."

I smiled. "But what will we do with it? Where are we going to put it?"

"Let us keep it somewhere for now. We may find a place for it some day."

He designed masterly abstractions, incorporating them in his architecture as early as 1889, in the glass ceiling light of his Oak Park Studio, in 1904 in the Larkin Building, in 1906 in Unity Temple and in 1908 in the Coonley House windows and rugs. A little later came the "City by the Sea," designed for Midway Gardens, which we now have in our Pavilion at Taliesin West. In that abstraction, kaleidoscopic and shimmering, he saw the multicolored forms of the city set against an intense blue background. Frank Lloyd Wright was truly the first non-objective artist, the forerunner of abstract design which soon began to appear everywhere. His abstractions, however, were always an integral part of his buildings.

In his love of ancient Oriental art, he believed it to be greater in its sense of the abstract and organic than the art of the Western world. People often wondered why a man so imbued with a vision of the modern world would "retreat" into antique art, collecting sculptures, vases, paintings, screens and Japanese prints. He explained this by saying, "I haven't seen contemporary work that I would put on the same level with that highest peak of Eastern civilization.

"The reason I use Oriental sculpture, paintings, bronze, pottery in relation to my own home is that they have the quiet, the depth and the sense of materials that you can find only in Oriental work. It does not exist in Western work. The Orientals are nearer to a natural architecture than we are; the Japanese culture came out of Japanese soil and Japanese conditions; even Japanese dress was according to nature—their nature. We cannot copy it, it is theirs, but we can be inspired by the way they did it for themselves. And we can do things for ourselves because we have learned that secret which formed their culture.

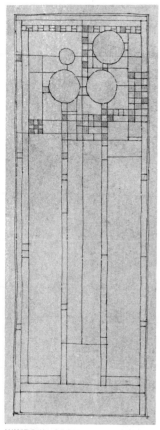

WINDOW, COONLEY HOUSE, RIVERSIDE, ILLINOIS.

SKETCH FOR MURAL "CITY BY THE SEA," MIDWAY GARDENS, CHICAGO, ILLINOIS

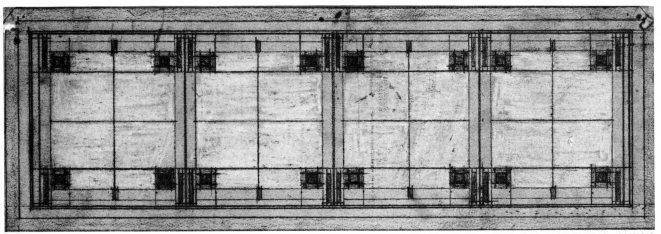

DESIGN FOR GLASS CEILING LIGHT, OAK PARK STUDIO, ILLINOIS

"Organic architecture was in possession of that secret before it ever saw anything Japanese. Form is to the life as the life is to the form. In other words, the nature of the thing has its own expression, according to the materials, according to the method, according to the man. And when the building is of that character it is beautiful, because it has the same quality that a tree has, that flowers have, that a beautiful human being has." When our friend, Georgia O'Keeffe, gave us her painting of "Pelvis with Shadows and the Moon" he appreciated every line and shade of its blues and whites. He also bought Klimt's semi-abstract painting of his mother, which he showed proudly to our friends.

He loved books. He loved William Blake, Walt Whitman, Emerson, Thoreau, and valued Samuel Butler in *The Way of All Flesh,* which he thought faithfully represented its era. In such novels, he thought, history was better recorded than in orthodox historical works. He often spoke of Tolstoy as the best representative of his time and especially admired *War and Peace* and *Resurrection.* He appreciated Dostoyevsky who, he thought, had best interpreted the search and indecision of those immersed in the wild passions and sorrows of the spirit that characterized his age. Dickens too he enjoyed.

Among the French novelists he read avidly were Victor Hugo, whom he often quoted, and Dumas, particularly his *The Three Musketeers.* Often he would refer to the characters in that novel, Porthos, Athos and D'Artagnan, as though they were people he had really known. "He has the elegance of D'Artagnan," he would sometimes remark about some friend of ours.

Of the American writers to whom he introduced me, among his best-loved humorists were Mark Twain, O. Henry, and Thurber, whose stories he liked to read aloud to me. He was always reading to me or I to him and we had many a hilarious evening laughing together. It was in *The Four Million* that he thought O. Henry best reflected his times, touched with sadness, a mixture of tenderness and tragedy.

When he was preoccupied in a book, he would vanish altogether, and when he emerged he referred constantly to the book he was reading, often identifying completely with its author and his creative process.

He cared little for the modern novels, especially the best-sellers, which disappear as fast as they are published. Magazines, journals, newspapers, he devoured at terrific speed, particularly when we traveled, but the work of great writers he read with slow contemplation. Literature occupied a high level in his life; but he did not connect it, like music, with architecture. "Literature tells about man," he often said, "architecture presents him."

In a statement for *Scholastic* Magazine in 1942 on some of his favorite books and music, he said:

"The books one has chosen or has happened to read are important. Everybody makes a more or less natural selection, I should say, notwithstanding suggestions or commands. And the book fodder for which we have a natural taste does most to feed us.

"The Arabian Nights fascinated me as a boy. Aladdin and his wonderful lamp—the lamp represented the imagination, as I see now—was one of the tales that never tired me. My father brought me Edward Everett Hale's *Man Without a Country* and that made a deep impression. I remember *Don Quixote* was with me early, almost as early as *Gulliver's Travels, Robinson Crusoe*, etc., etc. I read voraciously, so they said, and many books went into me, no doubt to be digested and forgotten.

"I should mention Goethe's *Wilhelm Meister*. I got to that through Carlyle, after his *Sartor Resartus*. I guess I owe Shakespeare a lot because of Carlyle, and Goethe "the great liberator." And I should be ungrateful if I did not mention Victor Hugo, the great modern in my boyhood, who declared for romanticism as a new freedom. He wrote the best essay on architecture I ever read. It is in *Notre Dame*. Viollet Le Duc in the *Raisonné* wrote the most informing book on architecture I have read. Rousseau I never forgot.

"In early manhood I was Meredithian to the bone for years. Am yet. And then I discovered Samuel Butler and William Blake. In Blake I found the source of the Pre-Raphaelite movement in England. Rabelais came along about that time. And Shelley lifted me higher than was my wont in middle life and strange to say I became one of Walt Whitman's admirers at about the same time. I see no chasm between Shelley and Whitman, though Whitman is much more with me now. So are Thoreau and Emerson.

"I have read the great Russians. They early went inside me from Tolstoy and Gogol to Gorky and Katayev. Lately, finding the Bible in print by Cobden Sanderson, I've found it entirely fresh and inspiring.

I like Carl Sandburg, Edna St. Vincent Millay, Ring Lardner, Alexander Woollcott and the editorial observations of *The New Yorker*.

Mine is a catholic taste which probably means a hearty appetite, and I find much to admire in books that do not touch my own work; when I get to those that do, I find too much pretended or missing, just as I probably would if I were more developed in the fields in which I am still ignorant enough to enjoy without too close questioning.

"But, to me, the greatest literature, after all, is not words but notes. Bach, Handel and Beethoven, sometimes the Negro spirituals, Stravinsky, Scriabin, and Jazz. Music gives me more now.

"Yes, I find too much pleasure in all literature, script or music, ever to qualify as a model of any kind. My son Lloyd once took me to task for swinging so wide an arc in my appreciation, taking it for a lack of distinction and discrimination. So here I make concession with an uneasy feeling that I have omitted to mention the most important, if incidental, book factors in my making because they were so thoroughly digested as to be utterly forgotten at this moment."

And twenty-five years later in his book, *A Testament*, he writes again of these and other important experiences, not only in books and music but in architecture as well:

". . . There never was exterior influence upon my work, either foreign or native, other than that of Lieber Meister, Dankmar Adler and John Roebling, Whitman and Emerson, and the great poets worldwide. My work is original not only in fact but in spiritual fiber. No practice by any European architect to this day has influenced mine in the least.

"As for the Incas, the Mayans, even the Japanese—all were to me but splendid confirmation. Some of our own critics could be appreciated—Lewis Mumford (*Sticks and Stones*), early Russell Hitchcock, Montgomery Schuyler and a few others. . . .

"At that early day I was thrilled by Mayan, Inca and Egyptian remains, loved the Byzantine. The Persian fire-domed, fire-backed structures were beautiful to me. But never anything Greek except the sculpture and the Greek vase—the reward of their persistence in search of the elegant solution. My search was more for the exception that went to prove the rule, than for the rule itself.

"As for inspiration from human nature, there were Laotze, Jesus, Dante, Beethoven, Bach, Vivaldi, Palestrina, Mozart. Shakespeare was in my pocket for the many years I rode the morning train to Chicago. I learned, too, from William Blake (all of his work I read), Goethe, Wordsworth, Dr. Johnson, Carlyle (*Sartor Resartus* at the age of fourteen), George Meredith, Victor Hugo, Voltaire, Rousseau, Cervantes, Nietzsche, Unamuno, Heraclitus, Aristotle, Aristophanes.

"I loved the Byzantine of San Sophia—a true dome in contrast to Michelangelo's bastard. I loved the great Momoyama period in Japanese painting and the later Ukiyoe as I found it in the woodblock prints of the periods. These prints I collected with extravagant devotion and shameful avidity, and sat long at the inspiring series of Hokusai and Hiroshige; learned much from Korin, Kenzan, Sotatz and always the primitives. The Ukiyoe and the Momoyama, Japanese architecture and gardening, confirmed my own feeling for my work and delighted me, as did Japanese civilization which seemed so freshly and completely of the soil, organic.

"Gothic soared for me, too; but seldom if ever the Renaissance in architecture, outside the original contributions of the Italians. I read, being a minister's son, much of the Bible; and inhabited, now and then, all the great museums of the world, from America to London, across the globe to Tokyo.

"I read and respected many of our own poets and philosophers, among them: Emerson, Thoreau, Melville, William James, Charles Beard, John Dewey, Mark Twain, our supreme humorist-story-teller; especially the giver of the new religion of democracy, Walt Whitman. I cared little for the great pragmatists in philosophy and less for the Greek sophists. Historicism always seemed equivocal to me; the best of the histories Gibbon's *Rome;* my respect for Frederick Froebel always high owing to my mother's kindergarten table. Soon I turned away from the Greek abstraction via Oxford or elsewhere. Of all the fine arts, music it was that I could not live without, and—as taught by my father (the symphony an edifice of sound)—found in it sympathetic parallel to architecture. Beethoven, and Bach too, were princely architects in my spiritual realm.

"I liked Beethoven's great disciple, Brahms. Italy was to me and is still so ever the beating heart of art creative, manifest in Vivaldi, the Italian troubadours and Palestrina. They came along with Giotto,

Mantegna, Leonardo, etc. . . .

"I found repeatedly confirmed that the inferior mind not only learns by comparison, but loosely confers its superlatives, while the superior mind which learns by analysis refrains from superlatives. I have learned about architecture by root, by world-wide travel and by incessant experiment and experience in the study of nature. In the midst of sensible experiment based always upon preliminary experiments, I never had the courage to lie. Meantime I lived with all the expressions of beauty I could see. And all those that I could acquire and use for study and enjoyment I acquired as my library, but living with them all as I might. I never had much respect for the collector's mind."

With books, as with music or any other expression of culture, he also needed constant visual satisfaction. He did not believe that the design of books had to follow orthodox patterns. A book must have beauty of proportion, artistic type-setting, a perfectly designed title. He was concerned with how every letter was to be presented and liked to designate the color of paper and ink, the spaces between letters and words, the page margins, and whenever he saw a book he liked he first appraised its format. "Look, Olgivanna," he would marvel, "Isn't this book beautifully made? Look at the texture of the cover. Look at the gold edges of the paper, how delicate they are," and because he felt that a book was to be treasured as an expression of human life and thought, it took him a long time to accept paperback books. He felt books should not be treated simply as a commodity, that the appearance of a book should convey its quality and distinction. This love of fine books remained with him all his life, and gave him great delight. Whenever we traveled, in the United States or abroad, he loved to go to the art galleries and antique shops where he would vanish into the rare book and print departments, forgetting the hours of the day. Once we bought so many books, sculptures, prints and brocades that we had to exchange our plane reservations for a boat trip back home from Paris.

He was wonderful to travel with because he felt at home in any country. And looking at architecture, he was naturally a severe critic, his appraisal always objective without any sentimentality. Of all cities he loved Paris best. "It is a well-planned city," he said, "beautiful, spacious, congruent." He enjoyed London too, saying that in its design it reminded him of a cluster of grapes, was enchanted by the "greenest green grass in the world," and loved the intimacy of English gardens, clustered with shrubs and flowers. Because he believed travel to be a great education for the young, we took our daughter Iovanna out of school every now and then to travel with us to many countries. He did, however, think that good travelogues and foreign moving pictures were educational, a helpful substitute for travel itself, and would never take time to travel for its own sake. What took us to France, Italy, Germany, Yugoslavia, England, Iraq, Egypt, was an invitation to lecture or give an exhibition of his drawings, attend an architectural congress or do some architectural work. Nor did he believe in taking from his work the time necessary to study foreign languages. He would say, "I am perfectly content to speak English well and I don't believe I speak it quite well enough as yet."

The highest expression of culture to him meant translating great ideas into action. I believe it was because of his faith in that ideal that he had such an acute interest in philosophy, literature and poetry. It prompted him to open every book with curiosity in order to find something which could be utilized for the best in himself. He believed that reading books on philosophy was most important, a point on which we met from the very beginning of our life together. It was the inner structure of life that he explored first and only then moved into exterior form.

Philosophy as he saw it was never in the abstract. No matter how abstract its expression, he utilized it in some imaginative way in his work. His architecture bears the image of thought and feeling and is eternally alive. When we enter a building of his we sense at once a fourth-dimensional quality beyond its three-dimensional aspect, some mystery in it that everyone, according to his ability, receives.

Of the twentieth century philosophers, he responded most to Unamuno, whom we discovered after the automobile accident of our daughter Svetlana. During the terrible months following her death, Unamuno's *Tragic Sense of Life* became our constant companion. He was impressed by the Spanish philosopher's profound search for God and by the nature of his assertion which was never dogmatic. Unamuno's passionate search and the way in which he carried it through confirmed the faith that man had a divine presence, the search itself the equivalent of faith. He especially liked this passage:

". . . The visible universe, the universe that is created by the instinct of self-preservation, becomes all too narrow for me. It is like a cramped cell, against the bars of which my soul beats its wings in vain. Its lack of air stifles me. More, more, and always more! I want to be myself, and yet without ceasing to be myself to be others as well, to merge myself into the totality of things visible and invisible, to extend myself into the illimitable of space and to prolong myself into the infinite of time. Not to be all and for ever is as if not to be—at least, let me be my whole self, and be so for ever and ever. And to be the whole of myself is to be everybody else. Either all or nothing! . . . The vanity of the passing world and love are the two fundamental and heart-penetrating notes of true poetry. And they are two notes of which neither can be sounded without causing the other to vibrate. The feeling of the vanity of the passing world kindles love in us, the only thing that triumphs over the vain and transitory, the only thing that fills life again and eternalizes it."

Frank Lloyd Wright's interest was not confined to the Western philosophers; he was absorbed in Oriental thought as well. Although he respected Hindu philosophy, he had little sympathy with the concept of detachment, its sense of a deity without feeling, mind or intellect. He leaned more toward the philosophy of a spirit which is self-perpetuating in its awareness, not merely dispersed as an unconscious force. Because he thought Hindu sculpture and painting too sensual in expression, he placed them on a lower plane and Hindu architecture was eclectic, not *of* the land, not organic in expression. Borrowed from Persia and China, it had lost the valuable vitality of the spirit.

Among the Oriental philosophers, Laotze was his chosen mentor; his understanding was heightened when he discovered that Laotze expressed his belief in the interior world of man, and he often quoted Laotze, "The reality of a building does not consist in the roof and walls, but in the space within to be lived in."

"It cannot truthfully be said that organic architecture was derived from the Orient," he writes in *The Natural House.* "We have our own way of putting these elemental (so ancient) ideals into practical effect. Although Laotze, as far as we know, first enunciated the philosophy, it probably preceded him but was never built by him or any Oriental. The idea of organic architecture, that the reality of the building lies in the space within to be lived in, the feeling that we must not enclose ourselves in an envelope which is the building, is not alone Oriental. Democracy, proclaiming the integrity of the individual per se, had the feeling if not the words. Nothing else Western except the act of an organic architecture had ever happened to declare that Laotzian philosophic principle which was declared by him 500 years before our Jesus. It is true that the wiser, older civilizations of the world had a quiescent sense of this long before we of the West came to it.

"For a long time I thought I had 'discovered' it, only to find after all that this idea of the interior space being the reality of the building was ancient and Oriental. It came to me quite naturally from my Unitarian ancestry and the Froebelian kindergarten training in the deeper primal sense of the form of the interior or heart of the appearance of 'things.' I was entitled to it by the way I happened to come up along the line—perhaps. I don't really know. Chesty with all this, I was in danger of thinking of myself as, more or less, a prophet. When building Unity Temple at Oak Park and the Larkin Building in Buffalo, I was making the first great protest I knew anything about against the building coming up on you from the outside as enclosure. I reversed that old idiom in idea and in fact.

"When pretty well puffed up by this I received a little book by Okakura Kakuzo, entitled *The Book of Tea,* sent to me by the ambassador from Japan to the United States. Reading it, I came across this sentence: 'The reality of a room was to be found in the space enclosed by the roof and wall, not in the roof and walls themselves.'

"Well, there was I. Instead of being the cake, I was not even dough. Closing the little book I went out to break stone on the road, trying to get my interior self together. I was like a sail coming down; I had thought of myself as an original, but was not. It took me days to swell up again. But I began to swell up again when I thought, 'After all, who built it?' Then I thought, 'Well, then, everything is all right, we can still go along with head up.' I have been going along—head up —ever since."

During much of his life, he was often called arrogant. He once said, "If you insist that I am arrogant, then I prefer honest arrogance to your hypocritical humility." But "arrogant" is the wrong word for his character; an arrogant man is never well-bred and he was first of all well-bred, strongly aware of the necessity of good manners, which had been ingrained in him in his upbringing. He explained good manners as originating in kindness and consideration of one another, and his definition of a gentleman was quite simply—"a gentle man."

What some saw as arrogance in him was his natural truthfulness. At times the truth does appear arrogant when it is not flattering, but that is only its appearance, not its content. In speaking, whether personally or from the platform, Frank Lloyd Wright was frank and direct, not arrogant. He would attack as with a sword a certain status of things he believed to be wrong, and if he did grow angry, he did so with a style that unbalanced jealous enemies, but he never knew falsification. For him the truth was the pre-eminent reality of his life.

I remember a party at which he met the editor-publisher of some well-known newspapers whom he asked, with a twinkle in his eye: "Well, when are you going to start a really good newspaper in this city?" The publisher was taken aback. "Why, what is wrong with the papers we publish? They are very fine papers."

"Well," Mr. Wright said, "they are tandem papers. There is no opposing voice here, and there should be one so that an entire town is not influenced by only one political philosophy, one approach to life. There should be friction, there should be the possibility of a variety of opinions, and I believe that your papers do not live up to that." This statement might have been considered rude or arrogant, but the tone of his voice was gentle, and the way in which he spoke was perfectly within the limits of good manners. He liked the publisher; he was only expressing what he believed in.

His consideration of others was singular. If, for example, we did not hear from some friend over a period of time, he would become very concerned. "Olgivanna, did I do something wrong, or did you? Maybe we offended one of our best friends. Maybe I did something he didn't like. Don't you think you had better write or telephone?"

"Of course there is nothing wrong, but I will phone. We've always been very nice to him. He's probably just been busy." And more often the apology would come from the friend.

The fact was, as I have often said, that throughout his life he placed the blame on his own shoulders. This is hardly the way of arrogance. An arrogant man is usually unaware, often guilty of bad taste and poor manners, and rarely questions himself; but Frank Lloyd Wright questioned everything he did, and he did not feel, as the arrogant man often does, that the world was hostile. The only time he hurt himself against the world's sharp edges was when he presented new ideas. It was only then that the world was hostile to him, although he never really thought so himself; the idea that he was confronted by an antagonistic society was more the interpretation of others; his optimistic force protected him from any bitterness.

He well knew how to sharpen a sword and slash it hard and high, but he did it really more or less for the sake of sport. Believing that there are few critics indeed who possess creative imagination, he held no evil in his heart even toward his critics. Usually the critic is one who sees only the material aspect, the body of a work, not its spirit, and therefore can never fully understand a new idea. So his view of critics in general was not high, but he had a few friends whom he genuinely admired, among them Lewis Mumford. But later, he felt that Mumford had forsaken the idea of this new architecture which he called organic.

A talk he gave one morning in 1954 illustrates the meaning of true criticism as he saw it:

"I often wonder how many have read George Meredith's *The Comic Spirit*? Not many. It astonishes me whenever I ask a question of this kind from the platforms of the United States about some famous cornerstone of literature which I call education or experience. George Meredith was one of my early experiences that I might call formative. The distinguished essay he wrote on the comic spirit is fundamental in studies of literature. Let us think of the critical spirit along similar lines. Who has a right to criticize? Whose criticism would one listen to with respect? Real criticism is not careless; it is not something that happens as a matter of conversation. It is not enough to allow people to blow off their top about something or other they may not like. I think the criticism we receive in our country now as things are is practically worthless.

"I doubt if there is much deep spirit in criticism such as George Meredith was trying to bring out in his essay on the Comic Spirit. The spirit is the reality of whatever you are regarding, or whatever may happen. Granted that the spirit is right, whence comes the privilege, the authority to be regarded as bona fide in whatever one says—or does? Of course, it is honesty. Criticism should be honest, never careless, and it is always to be listened to only from those who have a right to be regarded as superior in that connection. Behind criticism there must always be an experience.

"But criticism without experience is the mode of the day. What right do you have to assume to be a critic? What do you do when you criticize others? What is the act, the nature of it? It is an appraisal, according to what we think, what our experience is. The whole question back of criticism is: who is it that criticizes and what does he know, what authority has he? What is the spirit of criticism? We know what the comic spirit is. It is that in us which provokes and receives hilarity, laughter; but it is not the sense of humor. The comic spirit is closer to the ridiculous than it is to the humorous. And what is the difference between humor and ridicule? Humor has in it something close to tears; it goes deep into human nature. Ridicule is just that of the buffoon, something on the surface, much easier to practice. That is what we usually get in the name of humor. So it is with criticism: the critical act is always an egoistic act. To assume to criticize we immediately put ourselves above that which we criticize—or outside of it—and look at it and say what we think about it.

"But if we are to have real criticism, we have to look into the nature of it, deeper than what appears on the surface. And we must earn the right to our opinion by that knowledge which is, 99 times out of 100, missing in any professional criticism we read. There have been dramatic critics who practiced criticism their life long and never really saw or understood anything. But there are others—very few—whose criticism has become literature; they criticized with sympathy, appreciation, understanding. It seems to me we have the right to criticize anything only when we understand and appreciate and, knowing it, we wish to reveal our knowledge, to utter our appreciation; and to lay our appraisal alongside of others. A prevalent evil all through our society today is that little young minds are being led around, as though on a string, by what they read in the papers, by what this man says about that man. The columnist will utter his opinion concerning this or that or the other about some person, some occurrence, play or book, and do his best to show how superior he is to what he is criticizing. What makes the game fascinating, and even profitable, I imagine, is the fact that we can maintain a level above that level upon which we place the subject of our criticism. If we cannot look down as we criticize, we are not a critic in the generally accepted sense of the term.

"It seems to me that a man who can look in, no matter where he is, from below or from above or from one side, and see *into* the thing that he criticizes and reveal its nature, would have to have understanding of it, the understanding that is love. True criticism would only come from those who appreciate what they criticize. If we do not appreciate it, we have no right to criticize it. Let us say, then, that we condemn something. To condemn without understanding is foolish, and it usually has reactions that are pretty violent in the course of time and so we cheat ourselves out of something very well worth having. If we take the true critical spirit in the sense that George Meredith spoke of the comic spirit, as something to be had from within only and only on the basis of a sound and humane feeling—a feeling for the human qualities of that which we criticize—only then, I think, is it justified.

"Young America is filled with the critical spirit that looks superficially, condemns on the surface, cheats itself out of the deepest and finest things of life, and imagines it has a good time doing it. I think it becomes a habit too, the critical attitude is a habit. To stand aside or climb up aloft and look down upon the subjects we are regarding is wrong. If we are going to criticize, we must court our subject, we must know it, we must be aware of its depths and of its qualities, because qualities are all that are worth criticizing. It is easy to say all of this, and it is difficult to detect in ourselves the resurgence of the critical spirit as a form of egotism. As merely egotistical, I think criticism could be wiped out with great advantage for everybody concerned. But as an expression of understanding and appreciation, the more criticism we have, the better.

"Now what would be the difference in that attitude and the attitude that is prevalent and commonplace about us everywhere? It is easy to turn up our noses at something we don't understand and don't like, but it might be of extraordinary interest if we were to go a little deeper into it. So one should not be careless concerning criticism. It is wiser to take all criticism with a grain of salt and refuse to have much to do with the superficially critical person. He is the person who is not going to get anywhere. He isn't going to really understand or absorb those things in life which feed the soul. He is bound to become an inimical, superficial, sour member of the society in which he lives.

"Now in everything there are many sides, right and left, in and out. We may be concerned with them all or with any one of them but to be concerned with only one is stupid, if we are really to view a thing well. It would be interesting if we could take a flower or a painting or any object and expose it to all and discover how many could see into it rather than just see at it. This is a quality that has to be developed, like all valuable qualities in human nature, by practice. When we regard each other, the deeper we see, the more we receive, the faster we grow. The critical spirit is good only when it is the spirit of appreciation desiring to understand.

"Walt Whitman described criticism in this sense better, I think, than any poet I have read. He said that we should judge, when we judge, like the sun falling around a helpless thing. That means perceiving, comprehending, taking its form and revealing it; and only as we are capable of this kind of judgment can we be valuable as a critic.

"Most criticism now current is paid for and it is not only worthless but vitally misleading, too, to the young and uninformed mind. Doubtless a great many of the books, three-fourths perhaps of those that are written, could be rejected on that basis, as harmful. In this respect, everyone should read Meredith's *The Comit Spirit* and Walt Whitman on criticism. As for John Ruskin, the high spot in his criticism was in his definition of architecture as "frozen music," but that is extremely misleading. It shows that the old gentleman did not know what architecture was, at all. But it made a pretty picture. It is not good enough, however, to be able to make a pretty picture of the subject we criticize; we should not be allowed to get away with that. Ruskin's judgments I think regarding almost everything he wrote on architecture were superficial. And yet, we should remember that he wrote *The King of the Golden River*, one of the most beautiful allegories ever written."

A NEW SENSE OF SPACE

"Down all the avenues of time," Frank Lloyd Wright said in a talk to the Fellowship, "architecture was an enclosure by nature, and the simplest form of enclosure was the box. The box was ornamented, they put columns in front of it, pilasters and cornices on it, but they always considered an enclosure in terms of the box.

"That was before there was the freedom we call democracy. Now when democracy became an establishment, as it is in America, that box-idea began to be irksome. As a young architect, I began to feel annoyed, held back, imposed upon by this sense of enclosure which you went into and there you were—boxed, crated. I tried to find out what was happening to me: I was the free son of a free people and I wanted to be free. I had to find out what was the cause of this imprisonment. So I began to investigate.

"One day when I looked at the model of the Larkin Building, which I was designing in 1903, I saw that there was something tight and unyielding about it and I could not understand why. The whole thing was a solid block—in other words, a box. Then it occurred to me to pull the four towers at the corners, containing the stairs, free from the building and make them independent features to let the light and air in at the corners and between the two big piers at the front, in which were the nostrils of the building.

"So I did, and when the building was built those corner towers became features and stood there as a kind of enclosure of space. This was the beginning of the disintegration of the building as a box.

"In the Hillside Home School building, if you look at the living room, you will see that there is no box mass there, it is a simple thing from grade to coping and the windows are made as features and put against interior space. The disintegration began at Hillside, went further in the Larkin Building, and it went further still in Unity Temple.

"Then I began to get the idea. I did not have it yet, I had only the feeling. You can feel a great deal more than you know and you resolve that feeling into knowledge by way of experience. And then you know. I began to know what I had been feeling, and I began to analyze. As you know, I was educated as an engineer at the University of Wisconsin and was dissatisfied because I did not really learn anything. I went through the higher mathematics and descriptive geometry and picked it all up by rote, without knowing anything about it.

"But certain principles began to work in me that I must have learned on the farm, in contact with nature. The study of nature became uppermost in my life. I began to see what it was that was the matter:

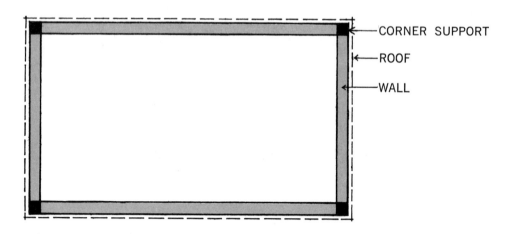

structurally, the box put the supports at the far corners and increased every span. The corners are, in themselves, dead to any use; there is the old saying: "put them in the corner"; the corner is always deducted from the life that inhabits the box. I was engineer enough now to know that the place where the building can be most economically supported is *in* from the corners.

"The cantilever principle is extremely simple: you put support in the middle, or you use a counter-balance. The length of the cantilever reduces the span and it reacts on the span so that the projection becomes supported at the same point that the span is supported. Structurally speaking, if you move the support in from the corner an appropriate distance, you reduce the span and support the rest by cantilever.

"Well, the principle of the cantilever, coupled with a desire to get rid of the box, began to work in my mind as a kind of miracle. Here is a box, now what happpens if I move the supports in from each corner? I have a very much shortened span and the corner, as support, is of no use whatever. What I really hit upon was a principle of construction that made the corner of the box wholly unnecessary. So I took it out! It was gone. It was as simple as that and the whole idea of construction and principle of architecture turned over in its grave.

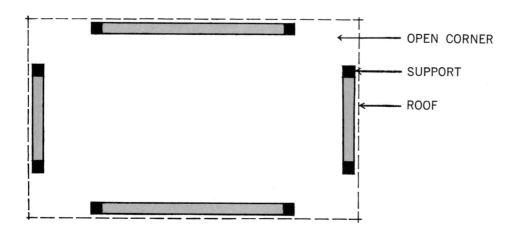

OPEN CORNER

SUPPORT

ROOF

"This could never have happened much before it did happen; it could not have happened in the Middle Ages; it could not have happened until we had the steel rod in tension. Nobody had done enough with it structurally to realize the value of tenuity in a building: that is, you could actually pull on a building. The ancients never could pull on anything; they never thought of tension in a building. But steel brought this new quality and now we could make a cantilever.

"It would not have done us any good to make a cantilever unless we had glass to fill up, and take advantage of, the open space created by the abolition of the corner. And now what happens? Instead of having an enclosure of the box, you have the free walls because the corner is gone. Instead of enclosing walls, you have a group of small screens, and you can play with them, the more you differentiate one against the other, the more you have a chance for freedom: the outside coming in and the inside going out.

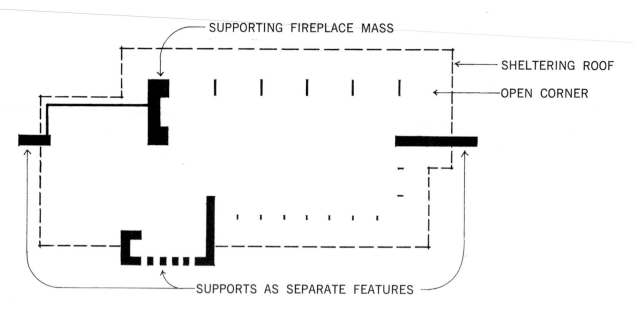

SUPPORTING FIREPLACE MASS

SHELTERING ROOF

OPEN CORNER

SUPPORTS AS SEPARATE FEATURES

"To go further: if this liberation works in the horizontal plane why will it not work in the vertical plane? No one has looked through the box at the sky up there at the upper angle, have they? Why not? Because the box always had a cornice at the top. It was added to the sides in order that the box might not look so much like a box, but more classic. This cornice was the feature that made the conventional box classic.

"Now—to go on—for instance, in the Johnson Building in Racine, Wisconsin, you catch no sense of enclosure whatever at any angle. You are looking at the sky and feel the freedom of space. The columns are designed to stand up and take over the ceiling, the column is made a part of the ceiling: continuity. The whole boxing up of humanity by architecture has come to an end. This idea is the basis of organic architecture, in which you have a new freedom of building for the human being. You can proceed in any way you please with the roof because

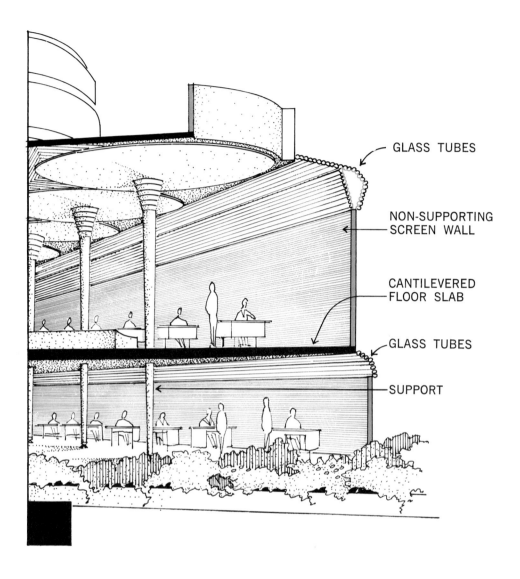

GLASS TUBES

NON-SUPPORTING
SCREEN WALL

CANTILEVERED
FLOOR SLAB

GLASS TUBES

SUPPORT

the roof, now supported as it is, can be constructed in various ways, even as a horizontal slab, independent of the corner—a new element entirely in the construction of the building.

"My architecture began to have freedom, gradually and conservatively at first. I began to manifest this idea, first of all, with the corner window; it became a feature of my practice in architecture, and it went around the world. You can see corner windows in Italy, in Africa, in Japan—anywhere on earth—but the *idea* behind the corner window never went along with it and has not gone along to this day. The whole ancient world of architecture disappears in this simple idea. There is no need any longer for much that architects have been doing for 500 years, which was merely ornamenting the box, building the box and then putting stuff on it and leaning things against it.

"Various freakish incidents took place. Michelangelo came into architecture as a painter and liked to work for effects. He took tall columns and put a big dome on top of them, up in the air; which, of course, was in itself an anachronism that could not stand there without some tension to take the thrust of the arches of the dome. The painter did not know that. What happened? The call went out to the black-smiths of Rome and they had enough iron in the town to construct an enormous chain which they got up there just in time. Chunks were falling from the dome and the whole thing would soon have crashed to the ground, but for the forging of that chain. That dome was copied later by Sir Christopher Wren when he built his building in London. But he was bold enough—he possessed quite a braggadocio anyway—to say that his dome would have stood without the chain. But everybody knows it could not have because it is pretty hard to beat nature.

"Instead of getting the effects from within the nature of the build-ing, they sought the effects from the outside; and that was the architec-ture we had in the Renaissance, and for 500 years later. The Renaissance never had a core, a philosophy. It was a backdrag of admiration for the times and the ways of the Greeks; it did not even go as far back as the Egyptians, from whom the Greeks got what they had.

"Now came, for the first time in all that time, the sense of the use of a new material, steel in tension, and the sense of the use of a new free-dom called glass. It is so easy when you know a principle to allow it to work for you and to create astonishingly sound and beautiful new ex-pressions. That was the basis upon which I have ever since proceeded to create effects. They create themselves; and there is no end to it, no place where they stop.

"It is just like the democratic principle that we subscribe to; that is why I have always referred to this as the architecture of democracy: the freedom of the individual becomes the motive for society and government. In the past, the individual was always considered untrust-worthy because no conscience had really developed in his breast; he could not be trusted, so he was under authority, and authority became God, so far as he was concerned. But that was abolished by our fore-fathers. With an ideal of freedom, being born free in a free country, the box got to the point where it no longer would serve; it was inadequate. And this is what is truly at the center of any adequate comprehension of what a building for a democracy should be.

"I do not think we should worry about architecture for authoritarian societies. They are not ready for this idea of freedom. As a matter of fact, they are not entitled to it; they do not make it; they do not perceive it because they are not ready for it; and they can still get along with the old practice of the facade. They are ready for the slab, for the monumental outline; they are ready for that, which in itself is like a monument set up in a graveyard. It has a certain impressiveness, but it is not *humane*, it is not of the heart. It is the old box, the old monumentality expressed anew. It does not matter how you stripe it, how you gash it, perforate it, decorate it; so long as that conscription is outlined definitely as a slab form, you do not have the architecture of democracy. You have the architecture of the slave to authority; no matter how willing he may be, still a slave. And that is why when we talk of the architecture of totalitarianism and the architecture of democracy being opposed by nature in form, we are telling the exact truth. Architecture can never be something apart from life. Architecture is not something a man does for himself, it is something he does because he is what he is, where he is, as he is. If architecture is not this, it is not great architecture. It is only the repetition, parrot-like, of something small and for small men—by little men, still after the effects. They do not have the power that would come to them if they understood the principles.

"In the richness and experience of a lifetime, ideas and principles working in the system begin to be a source of freedom and power to a man so that he can go anywhere, do anything he pleases, and sell it because it has to work. I know from experience. I had this feeling and it produced effects, but pretty soon those effects began to open something up and I began to get the secret of a power that will never leave me as long as I live. I never have to do two buildings alike. I never have to be held down to a pattern or a cliché, because this principle is so broad and so infinite a release, that I just could not bear to repeat.

"You would be the same if you got this thing into your systems to start with and it began to work. The core of architectural expression is organic; it lies within the building in the sense of space, and within that sense of space you become either one with it and blessed by it, or you miss it and trample it and go away without feeling anything. But the people who do that do not matter; they would never see anything anyhow; they could do nothing with the space of the box; they could only inhabit the interior space confined by walls. But now you are released by way of glass and the cantilever, and the sense of space which becomes operative. Now you are related to the landscape, to whatever is there you wish to be related to. You are as much a part of it as the trees, the flowers, the ground; you can pick up the earth and the sky. You are now free to become a natural feature of your environment and that, I believe, was intended by your Maker.

"An architect on this new basis becomes not only a student of Nature but a prophetic one, who can free his people, lead them, bless them, by what he will gradually come to know in the practice of architecture."

LIVING ROOM, WALTER HOUSE, QUASQUETON, IOWA

THE MIRACLE ON FIFTH AVENUE

In 1943, there came a commission to design a building in New York which was destined to arouse bitter opposition and to create reverberations around the world. Solomon R. Guggenheim, farsighted and courageous, asked Frank Lloyd Wright to conceive a building which would be suitable for the exhibition of twentieth-century, non-objective painting.

There followed sixteen years of incredible struggle against certain elements in our society which appoint themselves to destroy anything new. It is only human to be fearful of an unfamiliar form and when the plans were made public, objections were instantaneously raised by building codes, real estate interests, some architects and critics, who ridiculed the great idea because they did not understand its vast concept.

Solomon R. Guggenheim who had loved the design for the building and approved it for construction died in 1949. It was up to us now to fight for the revolutionary idea, a museum designed as one continuous spiral ramp with paintings to be hung on circular walls. Both friends and enemies alike thought that this building would never be built, but my husband, with his usual relentless force, never gave up his faith that it would. Because Solomon Guggenheim had acted slowly and over-

SOLOMON R. GUGGENHEIM MUSEUM, NEW YORK, NEW YORK

cautiously, there were rumors that he never intended to build the museum. We saw him often during that period and one day at a luncheon at the Plaza I could hold on no longer:

"Mr. Guggenheim," I said, "many are in doubt about the museum. It has been delayed for so long now that they think it will never be built."

He turned to me as if stung, stiffening his body, and declared indignantly: "The House of Guggenheim never goes back on its word—the museum will be built. You should pay no attention to what people say." And his blue eyes looked at me reproachfully. After his death his nephew, Harry Guggenheim, became the President of the Guggenheim Foundation. With his support and that of his wife, the late Alicia Patterson, the structure was on its way.

In my book, *Our House,* I described some of the problems involved in building the Guggenheim Museum and my visit to it with Mr. Wright a few months before it was finished:

"George Cohen, our contractor, and William Short, the supervisor of the building, escorted us to the Guggenheim Museum. As we drove up, it was a joy to see it softly glowing, perfect in form, expanding upwards in its spiral motion.

"Inside, the floor consists of circles four feet in diameter, delicately drawn with thin, metal lines. Mr. Sweeney, then the museum director, wanted the marble chips set in white cement, which would have been too bright and disquieting. But Mr. Wright insisted on grey concrete, which gives it a warm color. The horizontal openings at the top part of the walls beside the glass have louvers that can be pulled down according to the light required, giving a mother-of-pearl effect.

GUGGENHEIM MUSEUM. VIEW FROM THIRD RAMP

"We started our slow walk up the ramp. We felt as though we were moving on a level plane, and yet we were gradually rising. I had the feeling that the building also was moving up all the way into a cloud of delicate blue-grey light. As we walked on, the building seemed to expand and grow stronger till we finally reached the highest level of the ramp, which ended like a swan's curved neck. It is in this space, ultimate in expression of beauty, that the former museum director wanted to locate the repair shop for the paintings, thus denying the public access to the most magnificent part of the building. This fight has since been won. Also the white walls which were a threatening spectre have been given a softer color. 'White would give the museum a flashy, cheap, wallpaper effect,' said Mr. Wright. 'It will kill off the silver light that you see now reflected on the ribs of the glass dome which are painted a soft shade of ivory.'

"The ceiling is a crown webbed in metal and glass through which the light is molded into quiet geometric patterns. From the curved skylights above, the light streams down in soft delicate blue-violet shades

GUGGENHEIM MUSEUM. DOME

as though the sky itself were reflected on the walls. Therefore the walls appear luminous and throw light into the whole floating space with its great, broad curved lines which at one point turned into inverted curves. I felt as though I were standing on a shore watching ocean waves rising and falling, never breaking. All the lines flow, plastic in uninterrupted movement, one blending into the other. Two long pylons reach from floor to ceiling. The whole building is one with its parts as each part is one with the whole."

In October 1959 the Guggenheim Museum was at last ready for its official opening, the event I later described in my book *The Shining Brow:*

"Our party drove up to the Museum in several cars. The miracle on Fifth Avenue stood as a spirit from another world, glowing with golden bands of light moving upward in an ever-widening spiral . . .

GUGGENHEIM MUSEUM

"Familiar faces mingled with those of strangers looking about or gazing up in fascination at the great dome raised above their heads in peace and assurance. Space moved silently among the voices, lifting them along with its own motion, up toward the glass dome and on above the crashing noises of the machines in the city streets and still up—beyond the planes in the jammed sky . . .

"People spoke, one after another. Harry Guggenheim, Robert Moses, Mayor Wagner, Henry Cabot Lodge, Secretary Flemming, the Countess Castle Stewart . . . They spoke well, with the ease of professional speakers. Harry Guggenheim showed particular skill in handling the introductions.

"But the presence in the hall remained unperturbed by professional praise. And as we walked away the potent silence dissolved the voices into forgotten fragments of the past.

"We formed another formal procession outside of the Museum where Mayor Wagner was to cut the white ribbon across the entrance, symbolizing the opening of the building to the public. A solid cluster of photographers and motion picture cameras faced directly in front of us. They were calling back and forth to Mayor Wagner. The Mayor— holding the scissors—was waiting for their signal to proceed. He started to cut, the photographers moved forward calling out again for him to stop. Finally the scissors and the cameras clicked simultaneously. The ribbon was cut. A great mass of people stood on the street watching. The silence called to them to enter and partake of a world of beauty; a new vision into the future; a new promise for a better life."

For months, crowds in long lines on Fifth Avenue and around down the side streets waited for hours to see the structure that had aroused so much controversy in the press and on the air. The excitement caused by the building was unprecedented for a work of architecture, and now the public could see for itself. The response to the building was overwhelming. It turned out to be an ideal place for looking at pictures—"the liberation of painting by architecture" as Frank Lloyd Wright had put it.

People now come from all over the world to see how simply and beautifully this building has grown—as naturally as a tree. They come to marvel at the solution of a complex idea carved into concrete to express beauty and utility united—not opposed to one another.

Here is Mr. Wright's own statement of his concept of the museum:

"Here for the first time architecture appears plastic, one floor flowing into another (more like sculpture) instead of the usual superimposition of stratified layers cutting and butting into each other by way of post and beam construction.

"The whole building, cast in concrete, is more like an egg shell—in form a great simplicity—rather than like a criss-cross structure. The light concrete flesh is rendered strong enough everywhere to do its work by embedded filaments of steel either separate or in mesh. The structural calculations are thus those of the cantilever and continuity rather than the post and beam. The net result of such construction is a greater repose, the atmosphere of the quiet unbroken wave: no meeting of the eye with abrupt changes of form. All is as one and as near indestructible as it is possible for science to make a building. Unity of design with purpose is everywhere present and, naturally enough, the over-all simplicity of form and construction ensure a longer life by centuries than could be sustained by the skyscraper construction usual in New York City. The building was intended by Solomon R. Guggenheim to make a suitable place for exhibition of an advanced form of painting wherein line, color and form are a language in themselves . . . independent of representation of objects animate or inanimate, thus placing painting in a realm enjoyed hitherto by music alone.

"This advanced painting has seldom been presented in other than the incongruous rooms of the old static architecture. Here in the harmonious fluid quiet created by this building interior the new painting will be seen for itself under favorable conditions.

"There are many innovations in the building all on the side of convenient exposition and enjoyable social experience. Accommodation for the pictures, comfort for the visitors come to view them, their refreshment and social intercourse meantime encouraged, should they wish to have them.

"The paintings themselves are in perfectly air-conditioned chambers, chambers something like those of 'the chambered nautilus,' and are all well lighted by natural daylight as well as artificial light . . .

"Architecture, may it please the court, is the welding of imagination and common sense into a restraint upon specialists, codes and fools. Also it is an enlargement of their imaginations. Architecture therefore should make it easier to conceive the infinite variety of specific instances which lie unrealized by man in the heart of Nature."

FRANK LLOYD WRIGHT AT MUSEUM CONSTRUCTION

FOREVER YOUNG, FOREVER CREATIVE

In terms of creativity, as he proved throughout his life, there existed no age limit. His spirit was youthful to his last days and whenever he had occasion to be disappointed in his contemporaries he turned to youth for inspiration and reassurance.

Nothing pleased him more than to receive letters from thirteen- or fourteen-year-olds asking him how they should pursue the architectural profession. He always answered them. Between him and youth there was a spontaneous, natural bond; he spoke to them with love, understanding their plight as if he saw their future clearly and wanted to prepare them for it, not in a pragmatic, material sense, but in a creative sense, for the sustenance of their spirit. Perhaps they were to him the reflection of himself, for in his early years he was always in search of a better life.

He told me how in his youth he had preferred a friendship with a boy named Roby Lamp, whose legs were atrophied. In his desire to serve, he found that here was someone he could protect. This devoted friendship in his early years with a boy whose legs were paralyzed moved him to look at every youth with sympathy and concern for the future. It was a matter of constant regret to him that schools were not giving our youth what he felt was most important, the world of the spirit, the creative world. He believed that strong emphasis should never be placed on preparing young people to earn a living at the earliest possible time. He thought it unnecessary. "Draw from the source of inspiration within you," he often advised students, "and the technique will follow and the earning of a living will follow too. Work hard, discipline yourself and you cannot lose." He inspired youth to live up to the higher obligation within them rather than the mundane, which he believed would come along if the boy or girl were placed at the right starting point and shown the right direction. He abhorred laziness and procrastination. "Let them be taught to work with the idea that they are going to reach some great inspiring aim," he said. "That way their imaginations will be nourished continuously and they will always be productive. Don't worry them about bread and butter, don't make them believe that 'bringing home the bacon' is the motive and aim of their existence, it will be a natural consequence. 'The first thing is to get out and get successful' should not be made into an imperative postulate. Such an attitude will rob America of its future."

He would take endless time with a seventeen-year-old, talking to him as though he were a man of forty, placing complete responsibility on the youth's shoulders for executing his work, always with the aim of raising himself in his own estimation as a creative individual capable of facing himself, his society and his Creator without fear. Because he considered that the most important thing to teach youth is love of their work, he felt they should be helped in making sure to choose work they loved; and from that basis, everything else, including marriage, would then take place proportionately.

From his many talks to schoolchildren, I have chosen this one as an example of his inspiring message to them. It was given to the students of the Phoenix Union High School:

"I've had my faith pinned on you youngsters, teenagers, for a long time. I believe you ought to take your parents into your confidence a great deal more than you do. I think that this Capitol [of his design] for our state is going to be built for you and your children more than for the present generation. I believe that our sense of the beautiful resides more with you now than it does with your parents, your grand-fathers, your uncles, your aunts. You are the coming power that is going to be called democratic in America.

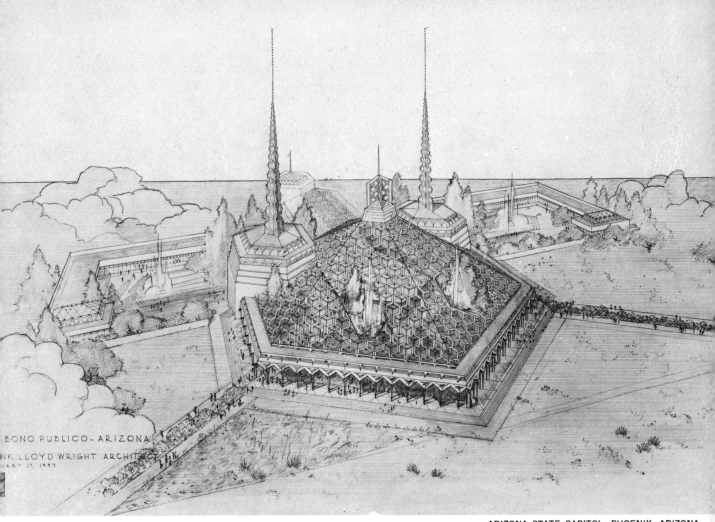

BONO PUBLICO · ARIZONA

NK LLOYD WRIGHT ARCHITECT

ARY 17, 1957

ARIZONA STATE CAPITOL, PHOENIX, ARIZONA

"About the problems which have been so neglected in your schooling—they were neglected in my schooling—we have to assert strongly the desire for the beautiful in order to get any attention concerning it in education. Culture and education are not on speaking terms now. That is one reason why I am standing here: because I resent the fact that architecture is the blind spot of our culture in America. And I doubt if one of you in this room has ever had any enlightenment on the subject of what is beautiful in building, what constitutes the architecture of tomorrow.

"Of what use is it to build a building for today? Buildings should last several hundred years at least. Now, we ought to be very careful when we build buildings; they should not be the decision of politicians who have axes to grind. They should not be the decisions of elderly people who have prejudices to maintain. They should be decided by the fresh young minds who are coming into life as a great inheritance and a great privilege . . .

"Now, you are the trustees of that because it is your children who are going to enjoy this Capitol, not your fathers and your mothers, and uncles and aunts. They look upon it askance, it is practically past now so far as they are concerned, but so far as *you* are concerned, this is *your* inheritance. Now what would be a guarantee to your minds, what would be a great Capitol for the state of Arizona? Wouldn't it be something that played in with the beauty of the state, that revealed the beauty and character of the landscape, which is so precious in this state, which makes it what it is today? Wouldn't it be something free? It would not be a sidewalk-happy building. It would not be something you could find on the sidewalks of every town in America. It would not be the urbanizing influences that are really going toward the end of a civilization, rather than toward the beginning of a democracy.

"There is the issue in architecture before you now, as young minds to decide whether the future is going backwards or whether you are going forward to the freedom which was promised by your forefathers and which we call democracy. Democracy has not yet arrived consciously at its own architecture. We are struggling with it, I have been fighting for it for 64 years, tooth and nail, I suppose you could say, because it has not always been pleasant where I am concerned, and it is not too pleasant now.

"I have presented you with what I consider a more liberal, characteristic, presentable future for this beautiful state than any sidewalk-happy design made wherever or whenever.

"If I do nothing more than awaken young minds to the possibilities of architecture as a great creative element in life, then I will have done all I expected to. I never expected to build this building, do not expect to now, but what I do expect to do is to bring home to you in Arizona the possibilities of a great architecture, a humanistic architecture that makes life itself more beautiful instead of a conscription that like a boa constrictor strangles you.

"There is the issue. Very simple. How does it appear in actuality? You see here a free plan. Here you have the House of Representatives, the Senate, and in the center a rendezvous for the people, called Arizona

Mall. It would seem to me that, in building for Arizona, what we call the free plan and the free principle of a free people should operate . . . It should have beauty and the life of the people should be dovetailed into the legislative process in a joy-giving sort of way. And you have a great circumstance here, in that the landscape and the features that are Arizona can be combined with a beautiful building in sympathy with it.

"Now, comparisons are odious. By comparing, you cannot really learn. The good mind learns by analysis. Go into each thing that interests you, study the nature of it, because all that is worth knowing in connection with architecture, or life itself, or philosophy of any sort, is the nature of the thing."

Such was the impact he had upon youth, through his written words, his talks and his personal contact with them, that they responded with tremendous enthusiasm, crowding the halls and eagerly asking questions.

One can see why they worshipped him. He always gave them inspiration toward an ideal that was greater than the usual warning, "Learn how to make money, young man."

"Think of beauty," he reiterated, "think of poetry, remember your spirit, consider your growth. These are the important things. You will be successful if you have the gift to pursue beauty. You will not have to push others out of the way or compromise or steal and lose your ideal. It is not easy to find it once you have lost it—the pressure of life is too strong by then."

That was the nourishment the youth of America needed; they reacted in an inspired way and in turn inspired him to renewed faith in our future. It was through this faith in the possibilities of the individual and the necessity to execute ideas with instantaneous action that he was possessed of tireless energy. He knew no obstacles. His principle was never to turn back; it extended even to the simplest matters. While driving somewhere, for instance, if something had been forgotten, he would say, "No, leave it alone. Go ahead. Never turn back." It was a characteristic that was active in him every moment. To him, the future was in the present and he lived his future, not only in his work but in every aspect of his life. Whenever he was asked which of his buildings he liked best, he would answer: "The next one." People laughed, but he was not joking. Once a job was done he put it behind him. It was always the next one that electrified him.

A quality of plasticity connected his activity in the present with the future. Whether it was writing, drafting, improvising on the piano, mounting Japanese prints, gardening, construction or social life, he never lost that quality. "You know," he told me, "when I go to rest in the afternoon and don't sleep, I relax and I am always designing something in the back of my mind. Behind my daily consciousness there is a sense of design ever present in my mind." He often wakened between four and five o'clock in the morning, alert, and made sketches of the designs which he had visualized in his imagination. He was a man who never lost time and lived every minute to its fullest; it is not surprising that he designed over seven hundred and fifty buildings in his lifetime. When people said he must have shaken designs out of his sleeve, he would laugh. He had worked them out in thought long before he put them down on paper.

He often said that beauty was the highest form of morality and sought it wherever he was, in whatever he did. The idea of organic architecture was the flesh and blood of his being. I know of no other architect who had this sense of his work as an indivisible part of himself. He saw the universe through architecture. He saw it in the structure of our inner world, of thought and motion, in the structure of all nature, and often referred to his work as harmonious or intrinsic, an architecture of inner harmony with the exterior world. The center of his buildings seems to reach out to an immeasurable radius where one is almost unaware of its termination; the lines, angles and planes flowing together in eternal continuity. His greatness grew from his understanding of the principle of architecture as it relates to the earth and infinite space. It enabled him to bring to life once more an art that had been moribund for five hundred years.

Naturally, he believed that one should never confuse the term "modern architecture" with "organic architecture" because the barren two-dimensional concept of the "International Style" produced sterile "machines for living" detached from human life. To him this was a misunderstanding of the purpose of architecture. He called architecture "organic" in which the spirit of life and light permeated every member and pore of the building, moving man toward an awareness of his true heritage. He truly believed that a beautiful building can help man dissolve the conflicts in his life, that a harmonious building has a quieting effect upon us and serves us as inspiration. Even those who speak of improving surroundings often forget that it is architecture, in its influence on the human psyche, that is the most important of all. If it were really taken into account by psychiatrists and physicians, they would not approve of hospitals built with rooms like cells. They would see that hygienic conditions can be achieved without the loss of humane proportion.

When Frank Lloyd Wright designed a church or any other habitation, it was with a concept of liberating man, giving him a sense of happiness rather than of oppression, refreshing him as much as a walk in the meadows; and because the human being to him was the highest entity on earth, he built to console him in the times of his tragedies and disillusionments so that by way of his environment he might experience a feeling of serenity.

FIRST UNITARIAN CHURCH, MADISON, WISCONSIN

BETH SHOLOM SYNAGOGUE, PHILADELPHIA, PENNSYLVANIA

"Architecture is the crystallization," he said, "the residue in some ways of the life of the time and character of the place, the nature of the man of that time—therefore extremely indicative and valuable—the only record we now can read concerning civilizations that have disappeared. We learn more about them from architecture than from any other source, and it would be true of our own period if we were to be destroyed suddenly. If the remains were to be studied by subsequent— if there were any subsequent—peoples, for various relations and effects, what would they find? What will go on record or be looked at in the future regarding this period in our growth as a civilization? What do we have that would withstand the destructive elements and forces that have worked down the centuries? Anything? Certainly not our steel buildings. If steel were imbedded in concrete, concrete would remain. Anything with steel exposed would just burn up and disappear, and of course all the wooden buildings would utterly disappear. But the plumbing would remain! Our porcelain tubs, closets, and bowls. The people of the future would have those, and they could read something from our plumbing of what we were. They would probably arrive at the conclusion that ours was the sanitary age. Plumbing fixtures might appear in future civilizations as parlor ornaments, the way we decorate our houses with antiques now.

"Architecture is not only the character but the frame of life; architecture is the structure of whatever is. It is the structure of music, of trees, flowers, stones, the weather. Architecture is profound; it is not a business, not even a profession—although they make a profession of it and they also make a business of it—but a great spirit of living in the whole of creation—basic. It is architecture that made the trees and the stones; it is architecture that made the solar system, the rotation and qualities of what we call the cosmos. All is architecture."

GREEK ORTHODOX CHURCH, MILWAUKEE, WISCONSIN

TRINITY CHAPEL, NORMAN, OKLAHOMA

His intimacy with nature enabled him to translate it into architectural terms. In the patterns of nature, the formation of a snowflake, a mountain, a crystal, a field, an ocean, a running brook, the indentations and lines in a jagged rock hanging over the sea, it was an inner beat, an inner rhythm he listened to, the inner character that he transferred to paper without ever copying or imitating any form, bringing never-ending variety into architecture. No blade of grass is a replica of another any more than a mountain is identical with another, and he grasped this individuality not only with his mind but through something much more complex; some call it extrasensory perception or intuitive sense or instinct, but it was beyond even these, a genius, cut in a different pattern from other men, that has appeared rarely in our history. In fact, history shows us that it has taken centuries to approach the power and vision of such men.

Even his daily life was marked by an intuitive understanding that often baffled people. He would talk to a farmer as if he himself had been born to farming; to a king as if he had been born an emperor. When he was introduced to the King of Iraq in Baghdad, the royal aide announced: "Mr. Wright, His Majesty, the King of Iraq." "And here," Mr. Wright said as he bowed, "is His Majesty, the American Citizen." He could relax equally with a hired man, a professional or businessman, writer or statesman. In talking to him you had a sense of his complete poise, as though in some way nothing ever disturbed him, no sorrow touched him, though much sorrow marked his life.

Many considered him a rebel. It is the precise meaning of the word that is important. If you rebel against disorder, staleness, ugliness, rebellion is noble. He was a rebel in a worthy cause, fighting against everything imitative and false. Living in a vision of the future, he could identify things merely expedient, architecture erected cheaply and grossly for the sake of profit alone. In the same way he rebelled against colonial architecture because it belonged to the past, against those who today, with all the advantages of science, still have recourse to out-moded forms instead of creating new ones. With nature in a state of constant change, he believed accordingly that change must be observed in the motion of time. He talked about this to our students:

"In nature there is a continuous ceaseless becoming. There is the great in-between, of which Laotze speaks, which is alive, which never ceases to be, and in that realm of being you yourselves will respond to that great sea of becoming. Knowing that it is all rhythmical according to innate principles and that if you can tune in on those principles to

CHRISTIAN SCIENCE CHURCH, BOLINAS, MARIN COUNTY, CALIFORNIA

start with, your hand will have direction and your mind will succeed in tracing from within yourself that which is there and alive and ready to be expressed when you call upon it properly. It is a moment which I think you could compare only with some deep religious devotion to a great ideal, to which you become subject.

"When you become a pencil in the hand of the infinite, as near as any of us will come to God, this thing that we call good design begins and never has an end. Because once you are aware of the importance of this understanding and contact with the spirit living in nature, you will never have to copy nature. If you want to do a tree, you'll do *your* tree, you don't have to do a pine or an elm. You may do a tree of your own. And you may do all these things on a scale and to an extent that would be bigger than nature that you see around you. You don't have to be the slave of that nature, you can be the master of nature because living in you is a higher germ of salt and feeling than can exist in the vegetable kingdom or the animal kingdom, and by way of it all these things become grist, you say, to your mill, and your own individuality—no matter how many of you there may be—will find its own fruition.

"We use the word fruition not in the material sense at all, but in the sense of true realization. In some form or other, the animals have it on a lower plane. The birds have it, the fishes have it, everything in nature has it, the trees, the flowers. We have it as a gift in a higher sense, as a spiritual quality which can make of life something more beautiful, more harmonious, lift it far above anything in nature. So, to descend to an imitative level in this process of design would be stupid— and yet it is what we witness almost always.

"There is another thing concerning this word 'organic' that's important. You do not divine organic principles inherent in nature by way of taste. Taste is, after all, only a matter of ignorance, which it seems difficult to make people understand; because the word taste is exactly what it means—you taste and you like or you taste and you don't. It is the same in the realm of the designer, the human being in action. Only by way of his taste does he go here or there or do this or that. The word organic to him would be anathema—the idea that there are principles that must be known in order to bear good fruit would be obnoxious to him and he would resent the term organic in relation to art expression, because to him it is a harness, a bridle, a regulation of the spirit by way of knowledge. Knowledge, at the same time that it is a liberation, is also constraint. It is like conscience. Freedom without conscience would result, usually, in jail—you would be incarcerated before very long.

"Well, so it is in the realm of design. When you sit down before this blank sheet of paper, you must have some knowledge and you must be guided by that knowledge toward an end which maybe is fanciful and imaginative, as you see it to be in nature. Nature never has to repeat a form—she hates to. She takes great pains to preserve a species, but she'll never cease endeavoring to differentiate the species. See the human race, observe animals, shells, fishes, trees and flowers. Never content, she will manage to preserve the species at all costs as you can see from her having implanted the sex principle in beings: to get variety, to evolute the species, to transcend the one pattern, to have richness of life which seems to consist always in differentiation, in individualization.

"I believe this principle to be inherent in the organic character of the universe as design, and in ourselves here as part of it, to participate in it. That participation in the depth of nature is really the world function, the privilege of the artist. What will make you an artist is the capacity to get deep into that sense of nature. So first of all an artist is a student of nature in that sense. He becomes that by way of his growth during the years of his endeavor, and it takes years, it is not a flashy thing. He becomes more or less a component part of that mind in nature of which his own mind is but a reflection. His own mind is only to the great mind of nature what the pine needle is to the principle of the pine tree. When that greatness, that sense of greatness of his function, comes to him, he becomes worthy of the name of artist.

"Of course we have been so far gone now by way of taste and willful performance and shallow pretense, the things that disintegrate instead of solidifying and upholding the good you are concerned with, that we have what we have today. I cannot see anything that is worthy of very great respect in architecture. We seem to have come along this line of civilization more and more bereft of this godhead which would eventuate into what might be called good design. And why? Abuse of course. You cannot abuse anything and get away with it. If you comprehend and strive to live up to the comprehension eventually, you will grow. But if we are satisfied, or let us say gratified, by a low form of self-indulgence—that is what has happened now in what we call freedom in our country—we miss the divine spark which might make us the leading light of the world today. I think it lies largely in this great constructive realm that we call architecture, which is structure. We are concerned in architecture with structure primarily, the structure of whatever is. Man's own structure, not merely as a physical unit—in that realm the scientist has us pretty well confused already—but as a creative existence in the world, a quality we know very little of. This is a kind of effort to see if we cannot somehow bring it alive again. It begins there with that blank sheet of paper, spread before you, and at this moment, when you are to invoke something within you which is akin to the great principles according to which you live.

"Now they are simple. And what are they? What are these innate principles that are existent throughout this universe of which you are but a minute, but an infinite part? We talk of integrity, of simplicity, of all the virtues, we talk of everything but this which is now inevitable if this performance of yours is to be innate. When we use the word 'innate' what do we mean? We mean, of course, something that comes from within. Has it been taught to you? Do you think you can go to school and find out? Where is this which is a revelation to yourself? I am quite sure that I am as much astonished myself when I sit down to design anything as other people sometimes are at what comes out. There is an element there which has to be in you, of you, and for the work that you intend to do.

"As you are in tune by way of your own quality with this proliferous prodigality about you of harmonious expression, which we call beauty, it is only then that you are able to strike out something on that white paper that really lives.

"What we call life we don't know much about. But it is there and as we are in it, of it, and for it, and faithful to what we can see of it, do we become designers. You have to relax, you have to let go, you have to allow yourself to emerge into a world vast and greater than you are to such a degree that the very relaxation, the very giving in, is a great blessing."

It often took a long time for the students to digest what they received. The quality of absorption differs, though not very much, but when the essence of the material we wish to absorb is as profound as his was, it is necessary to give it time to do its work.

I remember that often when we interviewed a prospective student who seemed rather drab and without much promise, Mr. Wright would remark to me later: "Well, he doesn't look like anything much now, but wait, give him time. You'll see in a couple of months that boy will begin to look like somebody." In the majority of cases this was true. After a period of hard work and concentrated effort, in which our young people were forced to think, to feel, to exercise discipline, an esprit-de-corps would take effect. Their appearance would change, they would begin to acquire a presence. Students learned at Taliesin that beauty is not excess, nor ever impractical. Beauty is a harmonious relationship of details integrated with the whole; and in a man it is a unity of the faculties he is endowed with.

With this concept, Frank Lloyd Wright never limited his work to architecture as a drafting-board process of learning, nor strictly to construction. His philosophy of architecture consisted of developing each individual to his highest degree in every facet of learning—literature, philosophy, religion, science, music. We encouraged interest in all these branches so that they might eventually become an integral part of everyday life. Fighting specialization at every turn as destructive of unity in the individual, he believed that architecture encompasses a world; properly understood and practiced, it contributes by its very nature to the structure of all of society.

This has been the Taliesin thesis; it involves broad study and because it involves integral participation as well, its quality is both universal and unique—as rare as a human being endowed with rich inner content. It is constantly generated by ideas of fresh inspiration, an ideal "university" where teachers have grown from the fundamental ground of learning by experiencing the principle of architecture, teachers who are themselves working architects and can impart to the student true insight into both the art and practice of architecture. Students and instructors are in constant intercommunication in their life and work, a goal which universities have been trying to achieve, but which is defeated at the outset by the enormous size of the usual student body. How is it possible to give students the basis for ethical conduct under conditions of a burgeoning overpopulation? This is what my husband referred to as "the flood, the trampling of the herd—with no hope whatever of really doing more than conditioning that mob. There is no such thing as enlightening them—how can it be done? What could you do in the direction of culture in a stampede?"

Thus teachers of architecture are usually forced to skim the surface of life merely, to pick up a few thoughts here and there from what they have had time to read, so they often discuss architecture on uncertain ground, writing theoretical articles and teaching students to erect buildings as temporary expedients.

I remember an architect who, having been bred in the "International Style," suddenly decided to change to the practice of Frank Lloyd Wright's principle of organic architecture. Overnight he wished to accept an entirely different philosophy. That being an impossibility, since it requires effort and study, he simply modified a few features of a house he was designing, leaving everything else as it was before he "defected." Of course, the result was a mediocre piece of work—a badly mutilated box.

The only worthwhile inspiration comes through dedication and experience. The pressures toward conformity, the desire for fame, the incessant demands of parents that their children earn a living as fast as they can, though they may become unscrupulous in the process, necessarily produces incompetent people. The world is full of them and the world eventually pays for them. Of course there is a conflict between our ideals of a merited high standard of living and a road to quick success with the compromises that often seem inevitable consequences. But it is truly not necessary to have "big money." Acquiring knowledge of how to handle money, how to get the best with it, and of course learning what constitutes the best, are far more important. But the conflicts caused when our ideals are confronted by our mundane goals often do confuse us. How often middle-aged men are apt to say, "I was young once, I had ideals then, but now I know better. I have become wiser." When a man acquires that kind of "wisdom," he becomes old without knowing it.

There was no such confusion in Frank Lloyd Wright's life. One of the most extraordinary things about him was that he maintained his ideals throughout all his life. He knew exactly where he was going and moved toward it with joy. Because he set himself many goals, there were many obstacles along his way and much suffering but he was able to transform them into positive forces through his courage and understanding. While there was work yet to be achieved, his spirit was radiant with life, and so his concepts of architecture constantly grew; and at the age of ninety he was young because he appreciated whatever came his way, kept faith in his ideas and fought for them. Although he criticized a great many things in the United States and vehemently attacked the desecration of the countryside, he was passionately devoted to his country and wanted to maintain it as beautiful.

I remember how grieved he was when he heard that craftsmen from other nations were not allowed to come to the United States, how critical he was about the fact that the crafts in America were on the way down: he believed that adding even more leisure to a man's time augured ill for his future; an excess of leisure was neither necessary nor healthy. Relaxation to him at home consisted in changes from one type of work to another, whereas leisure, he thought, usually led from idleness to apathy, often eventually to ruin. How pleased he would have been to learn that craftsmen from everywhere are now welcome in our country and that there is a renewal of interest in them here to make leisure more meaningful and creative.

Although whenever we visited New York City it was usually to work, either on a project under way in the East or on a book with our publisher, Ben Raeburn of the Horizon Press, we would go to the theatre nearly every night. He was never too tired to see a play but I would often be so worn at the end of a hectic day in the city that I would pretend I had a headache in order to stay in our quiet hotel suite for one night at least. Not he. His curiosity was enormous, his genius active in ordinary daily life. He had to know what the latest play was like or how good some new musical comedy was. If he happened to have a bad cold, he would say, "Let us go to the symphony at Carnegie Hall—it will help me get rid of my cold." And it usually did. He greatly enjoyed moving pictures too, loved comedies and laughed more heartily than anyone in the theatre.

Of course, we endeavored to get the very best moving pictures at Taliesin, and he never missed a single one. If he felt low and tired he would say, "It will help me change my thoughts. Let's go see it." Though some film may not have been particularly good, he always found something commendable in it—the presentation of character or the photography or the dialogue.

He was of course extremely critical of television, often expressing his regret that its great potentialities should be stultified by the pressures of advertising and timid sponsors. Again and again he would stress this aspect of the popular media and discuss their effects with our students. Here is a talk he gave to the Taliesin Fellowship in September of 1957:

"I would rather talk to a few of you here than talk on television to millions. And, I think, with greater effect—more worthwhile because we are a concentration and television is mainly a form of entertainment, is it not? Most are listening out of curiosity, not because of any desire to learn or with any feeling of conviction, either. But I think both those things are present here. How to rescue this great medium, which is becoming so big, from the degradation of the mercantile expedient?

"We have heard certain plans advanced regarding ways and means of devoting it to the people themselves without the absurd—like the barking in a circus at the tent of the sideshow—which is what goes on mostly. How do you think it could really be restored to a cultural agency in the interests of our intelligent minority, or even the medium majority? You have heard it proposed that the money for it would be raised by subscription and a reasonable devotion to advertising also, but not intermixed and interrupting and demoralizing the whole better element of television.

"How necessary do you think it is that every good, outstanding, upright devotion to culture should be at the mercy of anything—candle wax, toothpaste, aspirin, cigarettes, or what have you? How many of you would subscribe $25 a year, if you were asked to do it, to relieve television of its present degradation? Wouldn't all of you? That would amount to billions of dollars throughout the United States. At $25 from each individual listening, radio would be forever emancipated. And, inasmuch as we are so close, I think, to that emancipation, what agency would it be that would get busy now and plug for emancipation that would make a good television evening? It is going to be done sometime, but I wonder who is going to start it.

"They do have it in Bartlesville, Oklahoma. It only takes a leader, it only takes one or two—maybe not two, just one. Whitman said, 'Wherever there is the greatest man, there is the greatest city,' and that seems to be true. For instance, Hal Price, for whom I built Price Tower, an extraordinary man, an unusual individual, in the right sense. Now, I suppose that is the answer to what I was saying a little while ago. It will be the individual who comes up and promotes and gets established, gets the herd following in his direction and then we will have free TV. Nothing in America can live 'uncommercialized.' As they told me in Italy, we are a nation of merchants—the inference being that we are merchantable as a nation also. This is a deadly insult.

"Well, it is a great medium and if organic architecture could possess itself of the television it could go very far, very soon. I think we have never had, so far as I can remember, a real illustration of organic architecture on television. And our misfortune is that one cannot really show a good building because the kind of buildings we build defy the flat eye of the camera. We have not much advantage over the common garden failures when we are at the mercy of the photographers. The camera eye can look *at*, but it cannot look *in*. The significance of our work lies in the depth dimension, whereas the camera sees only a flat edge on a surface looking back at you. And that, of course, is what one finds in all the other buildings. So what peculiarly distinguishes us is lost by way of photography. That is why I have never been interested much in it. Everything I see is a disappointment, and all these years I have repeatedly heard people say when they come here to see Taliesin East or Taliesin West, or any of our other buildings, 'We have seen the photographs, but we did not know it was anything like this.' That is invariably their reaction. The reason, as I mentioned before, is that the camera has a flat eye and cannot discern what distinguishes organic architecture from the ordinary variety. If someone would invent a camera that would see into shadows and was rectilinear enough in a very wide angle to take in the whole building and show the terminals, as well as the snatches of facade, then I think we could score. Somebody in Italy said: 'Modern architecture is merely a system of photography'—something that would photograph well regardless of how well it was built and what depth of virtue it possessed.

"So here we are in a collection of new advantages, new ways and means of education, of living, of building, of being, and we have not scientifically really mastered any of them, certainly not the car, certainly not motorization. Flight is the most truly expressive success we can point to in modern development of our new advantages. The airplane holds the power. It is most satisfactory in the uses of the new sciences and has been the greatest benefit to us as human beings.

"If we average it according to what is most beneficial to most people, I suppose we would have to say the car. But when we look at the people who are controlling the production of the car we see the same iniquity that characterizes the whole nation at the present time and has it flat on its face: production trying to control consumption.

"If we get the cart before the horse, the horse can push the cart some distance, but not very far. And we now are in the rough of this most degrading era—production trying to control consumption. The big boys get together and manufacture whatever it is and then, somehow, by managed publicity, sell the product. They give money abroad to create purchasing power to buy our products when we make more than we can dispose of at home. Then we get the government to give money to foreign countries so they can buy our products. So it is pushing everywhere. The pressure is on in order that the production boys can sell their products and control the situation by doing it. Thus, the money flows into their hands and the power goes into the insurance companies from the people themselves and those red brick prison-towers rise. The whole picture becomes what we see today.

"I am sorry to say that New York City means to me just that picture of grief. As you come in you see all those fingers threatening the sky. Not one of them intelligently aware of the other. None of them has a plan, all pushing up from one real purpose—what is it? Why are they there? What do they represent? What does this great aggregation stand for up there, fingers threatening the sky? What does it mean? Is it a great tribute to our intelligence, our feeling, our mind? What occasioned it? What does this haphazard expression of might represent? What raised it? Crowding, of course. What opportunity did crowding give to do these things? Rent. Is not that great aggregation the apotheosis of rent? What is our wage system but rent? What is our money system but a form of rent for money? You can rent anything, even—the man. He can be rented too. I would say that New York City's boast, uprearing toward the sky, is merely the apotheosis of rent. When you begin to look at it that way and follow that thought, it does not take very long to arrive at the conclusion that the citizen, the human being, when production tries to rule consumption, becomes another form of rent himself.

"What does the study of Nature mean? It means that you take apart, see into and understand the significance of the forms that the eye takes in. If you study Nature and the nature of these things we are discussing, what do you come out with? That is what you should study, that is where architecture lies, that is where life itself lies: in a free democracy. You know, if you are going to remain free, you must be free by way of your conscience and your ability to think, or else you lose everything you have.

"To develop the study of Nature in that sense *should* be the office of education, but, if it were, would we see the sort of buildings we have on our city streets? Would we see the kind of men that are appointed as Regents? Would we see the kind of boys and girls that go out from good homes and villages to herd together and be conditioned instead of enlightened? I do not think we would. It is lack of the study of Nature that is responsible for this whole fiasco of the great idea—unless we wake up. What does America represent beyond anything any other nation ever came out, directly and above-board, to assert? We had a little of it in Athens, we had a little of it in the early days of Greek freedom. What was it? The sovereignty of the individual. Now since that has had its Declaration of Independence, which was what the declaration really meant, what are we doing in the eyes of the world to demonstrate the virtue of the practice of that idea?

"We have made a fool of the automobile for one thing; made a fool of the architecture that we might have had, for another; fools all the way down the line by way of license, instead of being guided by conscience.

"I am trying to show you the nature of what we call Nature study. It is not just studying the landscape, not just the relation of buildings to the landscape. It is not the study of the nature of building materials only. It is the study of your nature, the nature of what you represent, the nature of what you are for, the nature of the circumstances that brought you here. That is the study of Nature.

"Leadership can do a good deal, and that is what we have here at Taliesin. Leadership can open the doors and windows and let you see in what direction this work lies, and prod you on to make your own investigations and give you freedom and opportunity to be yourselves, at your best. And also at your worst. At your worst you become weeds and are weeded out. At your best you have good foliage and eventually blossoms, then you bear fruit."

MARIN COUNTY CIVIC CENTER, MARIN COUNTY, CALIFORNIA

GRADY GAMMAGE AUDITORIUM, ARIZONA STATE UNIVERSITY, TEMPE, ARIZONA

192

HOUSE FOR ARIZONA

1893

THE HUMAN SCALE

New sense of scale and space (the human being) to proportion all building. The human scale as a definite basis of measurement. Horizontal and vertical unit system in planning all buildings accordingly.

SIGNIFICANCE

New sense of the significance of the form in construction or of building-structure as a "form." Form arising from site and nature of the project, also of the materials and methods, always seeking organic or integral relationship of outside to inside and of both to site and circumstances within the building.

APPEARANCE OF THE OPEN PLAN

Integration of the building with the site. The dwelling as a gracious feature of the landscape and woven into it.

THE MACHINE

Various shapes and uses of material best suited to machine-craftsmanship and to modern methods of construction instead of imitating hand-work or any of the results of ancient slave labor or skilled handicraft. The machine versus the chattel-slave.

NATURE OF MATERIALS

The basic water-table striated brick and stone-work, low horizontal banded walls with broad over-hanging eaves, outside and inside same—interior walls extended outside to gardens, integrating human structures with the prairie. Stream-lined with occasional high emphasis.

THE EMPHASIS OF SHELTER

Substitution of back-band continuous-strip trim for plinth and corner block. Flush doors—swinging sash pintle hinged. The extended roof shelter with broad overhangs. The fireplace a manifest masonry mass of the building itself, instead of an applied feature of furnishing the building.

ABOLITION OF ATTIC AND BASEMENT

All furniture built in and designed in keeping with the type of structure to seem part of it.

FOUNDATIONS

The dry-wall trench footing. Trench dug not more than 16″ deep below grade filled with coarse broken stone size of fist. Bottom of trench to drain. Layer of concrete spread over stone-bed to carry wall construction above.

1896

The auger hole concrete pier or tapered punch-pile foundation on specified centers (spaced equal distances apart) carrying concrete slab on which building erected. These piles employed in extending walls around outside open spaces.

1900

Flat roofs for dwellings with projecting eaves; the reflecting soffit and the open or trellised eaves.

THE USONIAN TYPE HOUSE.
QUADRUPLE BLOCK PLAN HOUSING.

1894-1900

Lighting where source of artificial light is same as daylight. Reflected light from floor to ceiling. Concealed lighting on ledges, etc., etc. Pin-point lighting from ceilings directed on special objects and areas. Concealed sources of light. Elimination of the visible lamp.

1900

Flush doors: special hardware for swinging sash to allow screens inside. Pintle hinging for doors and windows concealed in floors.

The carport instead of enclosed garage. The kitchen as a workspace rising above roofs to act as ventilator for whole house. The extended lantern or clerestory windows for south-lighting northern exposures. Windows from floor to ceiling. The so-called picture window. All glass door and mitred glass. Elimination of the vertical corners of the box.

THE PRAIRIE HOUSE: Ladies Home Journal.

1903-1905

The consistent elimination of the post and lintel box-construction, designing the streamlined effects of plasticity throughout a building. New space concepts producing streamlined effects.

THE LARKIN BUILDING

The hanging or wall water-closet. Bowl suspended on partitions. No fixtures visible. First metal furniture, first air-conditioning, first pier and apron structure.

1911

The one-process wall: walls outside and inside same. Integral ornament. The nature of materials revealed in structure. The flat wood surface revealing grain. The machined flat wood trim strip. The designed sun pattern in building openings. Emphasis of the textures of metals, wood, stone, plaster, concrete, in all forms of building. The open plan. The split level floor plan. The quadruple block plan for housing.

1913

Integral heat. Floors warmed by gravity-heat: forced circulation of steam or hot water in steel or copper pipes embedded in broken stone bed beneath floors either of wood or concrete.

The balanced cantilever construction lightening loads by cantileverage.

MIDWAY GARDENS

First complete integration of architecture, sculpture, painting and music in America. Reinforced concrete construction.

1914
IMPERIAL HOTEL

The earthquake-proof structure. The resilient jointed structure on cushion-foundations. Tenuity as a structural principle instead of rigidity.

1920-1924

The sheet-metal cantilevered skyscraper with metal blinds. Water Tower Square, Chicago. The vertically divided skyscraper.

1921
USONIAN HOUSE

Various designs in varying types of shelter for dwellings in varying circumstances and changing climates either built by the Usonian Automatic Block construction method abolishing skilled labor entirely or in the nature of materials. All appurtenance systems prefabricated in shops and installed ready-made complete.

CONCRETE BLOCK

Concrete textile block construction. Reinforced concrete. Walls same inside as outside. No skilled labor. Fireproof, earthquake-proof, vermin-proof. Gravel, sand, cement, steel rods and common labor.
Textile-block houses: first use of the then gutter-snipe of the building industry—the concrete block now reinforced by steel—for high class building construction.

Natural top-lighted show window.

1924

The self-cleaning building. The outward inclined glass wall. Mitred glass corner-windows.

1933
BROADACRE MODELS

Decentralization. Models of Broadacre City. Plans and various models for orderly decentralization of cities. The universal four-way traffic intersection. Traffic solutions by way of designs for motor car, taxi cab, aerorotor and skidrail transport.

1912-1934
THE MODERN THEATRE

Integral sound. Visible sound-track on projection apparatus. Incorporated sound projection reflecting surfaces of building. Sound apparatus built in. The modern theatre itself as a modern machine for sound reception and projection. New elements in acoustics where dependent upon building construction.

The sheet-metal general purpose farmstead for northern climate. Detail of Broadacre City.

1936

The all-steel house, roofs, walls and floors.

JOHNSON BUILDING

Cold drawn mesh reinforcement for slender columns, walls or slabs in building construction sometimes expanding into cantilevered ceilings from columns or walls. Upper corner of box finally eliminated.

1940

Pool divided between indoors and outdoors.

1947

The meeting-house as an overall temple without steeple.

1953

The quadruple skyscraper on four pins with dwellings and offices vertically combined. Sheltered glass-walls. Cantilever construction. All floors cantilevered over central supports carrying floors. Building construction from within outward.

—Frank Lloyd Wright, 1953

ORGANIC ARCHITECTURE CONTINUES

"... freedom and opportunity to be yourselves. ... At your best you have good foliage and eventually blossoms, then you bear fruit."—F.Ll.W.

WORK BY THE TALIESIN ASSOCIATED ARCHITECTS

PLAUT HOUSE, MADISON, WISCONSIN. DESIGNED BY WILLIAM WES-
LEY PETERS, CHIEF ARCHITECT, TALIESIN ASSOCIATED ARCHITECTS.

LINCOLN INCOME LIFE INSURANCE CO., LOUISVIL
KENTUCKY. DESIGNED BY WILLIAM WESLEY PETE

LESCOHIER-KLOEPPER HOUSE (REMODELLED BARN), MADI-
SON, WISCONSIN. DESIGNED BY WILLIAM WESLEY PETERS.

ASCENSION LUTHERAN CHURCH, SCOTTSDALE, ARIZONA. DESIGNED BY WILLIAM WESLEY PETERS.

HOUSE FOR ARIZONA. DESIGNED BY ANTHONY PUTTNAM

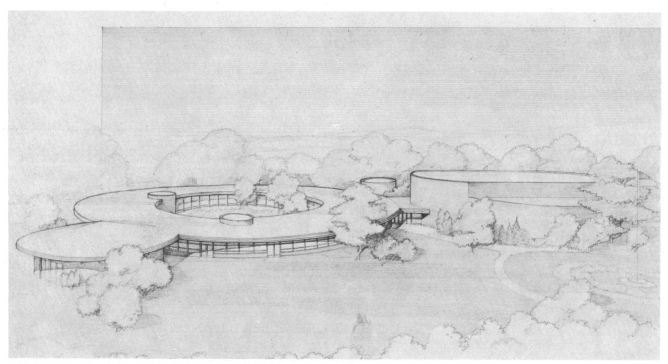

THE PRAIRIE SCHOOL, RACINE, WISCONSIN. DESIGNED BY CHARLES MONTOOTH

200

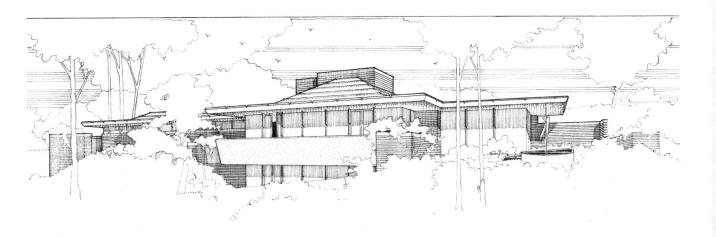

CHATHAM HOUSE, BETHESDA, MARYLAND. DESIGNED BY VERNON SWABACK

HOUSE FOR NEW JERSEY. DESIGNED BY JOHN RATTENBURY

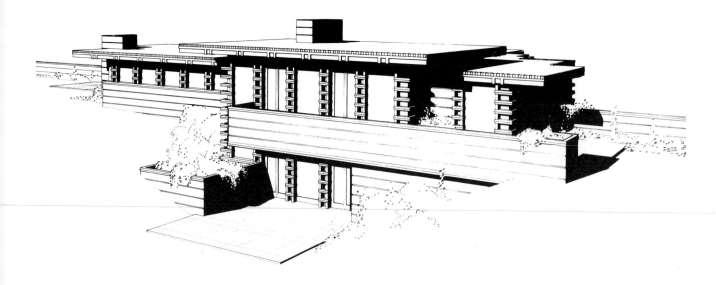

KRUM HOUSE, POLK COUNTY, MINNESOTA. DESIGNED BY AUBREY BANKS

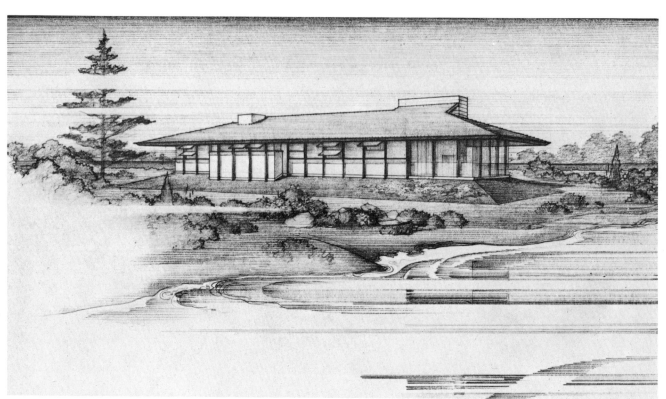

BURCHER HOUSE, POQUOSON, VIRGINIA. DESIGNED BY LING PO

HOUSE FOR WISCONSIN. DESIGNED BY ALLEN LAPE DAVISON

HOUSE FOR OHIO. DESIGNED BY JOHN deKOVEN HILL

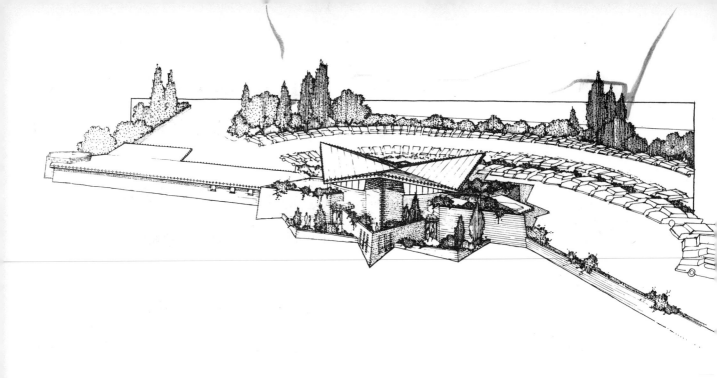

DELANO MORTUARY CHAPEL, FOR MR. AND MRS. CECIL B. LaCOURSE
DELANO, CALIFORNIA. DESIGNED BY WILLIAM WESLEY PETERS

ADMINISTRATION BUILDING AND VISITORS' CENTER FOR ROCKY MOUNTAIN
NATIONAL PARK, COLORADO. DESIGNED BY EDMUND THOMAS CASEY

THE BUILDINGS AND PROJECTS
OF FRANK LLOYD WRIGHT

Research by The Frank Lloyd Wright Foundation
Edited by Bruce Brooks Pfeiffer
under the supervision of Olgivanna Lloyd Wright

Introductory note:

The dates of the significant events in the life of Frank Lloyd Wright have been drawn from the Taliesin archives, mainly from Mr. Wright's unpublished manuscripts and letters.

Previous catalogues, both published and unpublished, contain certain discrepancies in dates assigned to Mr. Wright's work. In the following chronology the dates given to his architectural designs are those that most closely refer to the time of their conception. Where preliminary presentation drawings carry Mr. Wright's signature and date in his red square, that date has been selected.

Through the research by the Frank Lloyd Wright Foundation of many thousands of drawings and documents, this listing includes hitherto unknown projects.

Executed works are listed in SMALL CAPS and other works are denoted in *italics*.

1869

Born in Richland Center, Wisc., on June 8 to William Russell Cary Wright and Anna Lloyd Jones Wright.

1874

Family moved to Weymouth, Mass.

1876

Family visited Centennial Exposition in Philadelphia; discovered Froebel Kindergarten "Gifts."

1877

Family returned to Wisconsin, lived in Madison. F.Ll.W. spent summer on farm of James Lloyd Jones (Uncle James) at Spring Green, Wisc.

1885

William Wright left family.

F.Ll.W. entered University of Wisconsin as student of civil engineering. Worked for Allen Conover as junior draftsman. Developed drawings for University Avenue Power House, Madison, Wisc.

1887

Collapse of Wisconsin State Capitol Building in Madison.

Study for residence made while at University of Wisconsin (v. Henry N. Cooper, 1890).

Left school and home. Went to Chicago to find job with an architect. Worked at office of J.L. Silsbee; met Cecil Corwin. While at Silsbee's office:

    HILLSIDE HOME SCHOOL, Building #1, for the Misses Lloyd Jones, Spring Green, Wisc. (Demolished 1950.)

    Lloyd Jones, Misses, residence, Spring Green, Wisc.

    Unitarian Chapel, Sioux City, Iowa.

Left Silsbee's office; prepared set of drawings to show to Louis H. Sullivan. Accepted into the firm of Adler & Sullivan.

1889

Married Catherine Lee Tobin. Six children: Lloyd, John, Catherine, Frances, David, Llewellyn.

Became head of Planning and Designing Department of Adler & Sullivan.

    WRIGHT, Frank Lloyd, residence, Oak Park, Ill.

1890

Adler & Sullivan accepted few commissions for residences, most of their work being auditoriums and opera houses. Residential commissions they turned over to F.Ll.W.:

    CHARNLEY, James, residence, Ocean Springs, Miss.

    MAC HARG, W. S., residence, Chicago, Ill.

    SULLIVAN, Louis H., residence, Ocean Springs, Miss.

Cooper, Henry N., residence, La Grange, Ill. (v. 1887).

1891

    CHARNLEY, James, residence, Chicago, Ill.

1892

To support his growing family, F.Ll.W. accepted commissions (on his own time and outside of office hours) for several houses (e.g., Harlan, McArthur, Blossom). When Louis Sullivan became aware of this, he felt it constituted a division of interests. F.Ll.W. decided at this time to leave the firm (v. 1893).

The Harlan residence of this year was considered by F.Ll.W. as the beginning of his own architectural practice, although the house was designed while he was with Adler & Sullivan.

    BLOSSOM, George, residence, Chicago, Ill.

    CLARK, W. Irving, residence, La Grange, Ill. (Possibly done in collaboration with another Adler & Sullivan draftsman.)

    EMMOND, Robert G., residence, La Grange, Ill.

    GALE, Mrs. Thomas H., residence, Oak Park, Ill.

    HARLAN, Dr. Allison H., residence, Chicago, Ill.

    MC ARTHUR, Warren, residence, Chicago, Ill.

    PARKER, R. P., residence, Oak Park, Ill.

    SULLIVAN, Albert W., residence, Chicago, Ill.

    VICTORIA HOTEL, remodelling, Chicago Heights, Ill.

1893

Left office of Adler & Sullivan. In fall of 1893, opened his own office with Cecil Corwin in the Schiller Building, an Adler & Sullivan opus, in Chicago, Ill. First client: William H. Winslow.

    BOATHOUSE, for Lake Mendota, Madison, Wisc.

    GALE, Walter M., residence, Oak Park, Ill.

    LAMP, Robert M., cottage, Lake Mendota, Wisc.

    WINSLOW, William H., residence, River Forest, Ill.

    WRIGHT, Frank Lloyd, playroom addition, Oak Park, Ill.

    Boathouse for Lake Monona, Madison, Wisc.

    Library and Museum, competition drawing, Milwaukee, Wisc.

1894

Wrote and read lecture: "The Architect and The Machine." Wrote and read famous Hull House lecture: "The Art and Craft of The Machine." Exhibition at Chicago Architectural Club.

    BAGLEY, Frederick, residence, Hinsdale, Ill.

    BASSETT, Dr. H. W., remodelling, Oak Park, Ill.

    GOAN, Peter, residence, La Grange, Ill.

ROLOSON, Robert W., apartments, Chicago, Ill.
WOOLEY, Francis, residence, Chicago, Ill.
Concrete Monolithic Bank, early study.
Goan, Orrin S., residence, La Grange, Ill.
McAfee, A. C., residence, Chicago, Ill.

1895

FRANCIS APARTMENTS, for Terre Haute Trust Co., Chicago, Ill.
FRANCISCO TERRACE, apartment building for Edward C. Waller, Chicago, Ill.
MOORE, Nathan G., residence, Oak Park, Ill.
WALLER, Edward C., apartments, Chicago, Ill.
WILLIAMS, Chauncey L., residence, River Forest, Ill.
WRIGHT, Frank Lloyd, studio, Oak Park, Ill.
YOUNG, H. R., alterations, Oak Park, Ill.
Amusement Park, project for Warren McArthur, Wolf Lake, Ill.
Baldwin, Jesse, residence, Oak Park, Ill.
Lexington Terrace, apartment building project for Edward C. Waller, Chicago, Ill.
Luxfer Prism Co., skyscraper, Chicago, Ill.

1896

Designed format for *House Beautiful* and printed it with W. H. Winslow in rare limited edition of 90 copies. Wrote and read lecture: "Architecture, Architect and Client." Wrote "Work Song." (Music composed by Mrs. Frank Lloyd Wright in 1932.)
Cecil Corwin left office firm.
GOODRICH, H. C., residence, Oak Park, Ill.
HELLER, Isador, residence, Chicago, Ill.
ROBERTS, Charles E., stable, Oak Park, Ill.
ROBERTS, Charles E., remodelling, Oak Park, Ill.
ROMEO AND JULIET WINDMILL TOWER, for Hillside Home School, Spring Green, Wisc.
Devin, Mrs. David, residence, Chicago, Ill.
Perkins, Robert, apartment, Chicago, Ill.
Roberts, Charles E., four houses, Ridgeland, Ill.

1897

Moved office to Steinway Hall, Chicago, Ill.
FURBECK, George, residence, Oak Park, Ill.
WALLIS, Henry, boathouse, Lake Delavan, Wisc.
All Souls Building, Lincoln Center, Chicago, Ill. (v. 1900)
Factory Building, for Chicago Screw Co., Chicago, Ill.

1898

Exhibition at Chicago Architectural Club.
FURBECK, Rollin, residence, Oak Park, Ill.
RIVER FOREST GOLF CLUB, River Forest, Ill.

SMITH, George W., residence, Oak Park, Ill.
Mozart Gardens, restaurant remodelling for David Meyer, Chicago, Ill.
Waller, Edward C., residence, River Forest, Ill.

1899

Exhibition at Chicago Architectural Club.
HUSSER, Joseph, residence, Chicago, Ill.
WALLER, Edward C., remodelling, River Forest, Ill.
Cheltenham Beach Resort, for Edward C. Waller and Norman B. Ream, near Chicago, Ill.
Eckhart, Robert, residence, River Forest, Ill.
Residence (published in *Architectural Review*, June 1900)

1900

Wrote and read: "The Architect." Wrote and read: "A Philosophy of Fine Art." Wrote and read: "What is Architecture?" Wrote article on Japanese prints and the culture of Japan. Exhibition at Chicago Architectural Club.
ADAMS, Jesse, residence, Longwood, Ill.
ADAMS, William, residence, Chicago, Ill.
BRADLEY, B. Harley, residence, Kankakee, Ill.
DANA, Susan Lawrence, residence, Springfield, Ill.
FOSTER, S. A., residence, Chicago, Ill.
GOODSMITH, Dr., residence, Lake Delavan, Wisc.
HICKOX, Warren, residence, Kankakee, Ill.
PITKIN, E. H., lodge, Desbarats, Ont., Canada
WALLIS, Henry, residence, Lake Delavan, Wisc.
Abraham Lincoln Center, Chicago, Ill.
Foster, S. A., summer cottage, near Chicago, Ill.
"Home in a Prairie Town," published in *Ladies Home Journal*.
Little, Francis W., residence (scheme #1), Peoria, Ill.
Motion Picture Theater, Los Angeles, Calif.
School House, for Crosbyton, Tex.
"A Small House With Lots of Rooms in It," published in *Ladies Home Journal*

1901

Exhibition at Chicago Architectural Club.
The prairie house type had reached full development by the time the Willits house was built, expressing the new concept of organic architecture as outlined by F.Ll.W. in *An Autobiography*.
DAVENPORT, E. Arthur, residence, River Forest, Ill.
EXHIBITION PAVILION, for Universal Portland Cement Co., Buffalo, N. Y.
HENDERSON, F. B., residence, Elmhurst, Ill.
HILLS, E. R., remodelling, Oak Park, Ill.
JONES, Fred B., residence, boathouse, gate-lodge, Lake Delavan, Wisc.

RIVER FOREST GOLF CLUB, additions, River Forest, Ill.

THOMAS, Frank, residence, Oak Park, Ill.

WALLER, Edward C., gatehouse, gardener's cottage, River Forest, Ill.

WALLIS, Henry, remodelling of gate lodge, Lake Delavan, Wisc.

WILDER, T., stables, Elmhurst, Ill.

WILLITS, Ward W., residence, Highland Park, Ill.

1902

Exhibition at Chicago Architectural Club.

FRICKE, William G., residence, Oak Park, Ill.

GERTS, George E., double residence, Whitehall, Mich.

GERTS, Walter, residence, Whitehall, Mich.

HEURTLEY, Arthur, remodelling, Marquette Island, Mich.

HEURTLEY, Arthur, residence, Oak Park, Ill.

HILLSIDE HOME SCHOOL, Building #2, for the Misses Lloyd Jones, Spring Green, Wisc.

LITTLE, Francis W., residence (scheme #2), Peoria, Ill.

ROSS, Charles S., residence, Lake Delavan, Wisc.

SPENCER, George W., residence, Lake Delavan, Wisc.

Lake Delavan Yacht Club, Lake Delavan, Wisc.

Metzger, Victor, residence, Ont., Canada

Mosher, John A., residence

Residence, for Oak Park, Ill.

Waller, Edward C., residence (scheme #1), Charlevoix, Mich.

Yahara Boat Club, Madison, Wisc.

1903

BARTON, George, residence, Buffalo, N. Y.

FREEMAN, W. H., residence, Hinsdale, Ill.

LARKIN CO., administration building, Buffalo, N.Y. (First use of air conditioning, plate glass, metal furniture.)

MARTIN, W. E., residence, Oak Park, Ill.

SCOVILLE PARK FOUNTAIN, Oak Park, Ill.

WALSER, J., Jr., residence, Chicago, Ill.

Chicago & Northwestern Railway Stations, for suburban Chicago, Ill.

Lamp, Robert M., residence (scheme #1), Madison, Wisc.

Roberts, Charles E., Quadruple Block Plan (twenty-four houses), Oak Park, Ill.

Waller, Edward C., residence (scheme #2), Charlevoix, Mich.

Wright, Frank Lloyd, studio-residence, Oak Park, Ill.

1904

CHENEY, Edwin H., residence, Oak Park, Ill.

GALE, Mrs. Thomas H., residence, Oak Park, Ill.

LAMP, Robert M., residence (scheme #2), Madison, Wisc.

MARTIN, Darwin D., residence, conservatory, Buffalo, N. Y.

Baldwin, Hiram, residence (scheme #1), Kenilworth, Ill.

Bank Building, for Frank L. Smith (scheme #1), Dwight, Ill.

Clarke, Robert D., residence, Peoria, Ill.

Residence, Highland Park, Ill.

Scudder, J. A., residence, Desbarats, Ont., Canada

Ullman, H. J., residence, Oak Park, Ill.

Workmen's Rowhouses, for Larkin Co., Buffalo, N. Y.

1905

ADAMS, Mary M. W., residence, Highland Park, Ill.

BALDWIN, Hiram, residence (scheme #2), Kenilworth, Ill.

BANK BUILDING, for Frank L. Smith (scheme #2), Dwight, Ill.

BROWN, Charles E., residence, Evanston, Ill.

E-Z POLISH FACTORY, for Darwin D. Martin, Chicago, Ill.

GILPIN, T. E., residence, Oak Park, Ill.

GLASNER, W. A., residence, Glencoe, Ill.

HARDY, Thomas P., residence, Racine, Wisc.

HEATH, W. R., residence, Buffalo, N. Y.

JOHNSON, A. P., residence, Lake Delavan, Wisc.

LAWRENCE MEMORIAL LIBRARY, interior, Springfield, Ill.

ROOKERY BUILDING, remodelled entrance lobbies and balcony-court, Chicago, Ill.

UNITY TEMPLE, Oak Park, Ill. (The first great expression of the destruction of the box.)

Barnes, Charles W., residence, McCook, Neb.

House on a Lake

Varnish Factory, for Darwin D. Martin

Concrete Apartment Building, for Warren McArthur, Chicago, Ill.

Moore, Nathan G., pergola and pavilion, Oak Park, Ill.

1906

F.Ll.W. made first trip to Japan with his clients, Mr. and Mrs. Ward W. Willits. Began collection of Japanese prints and Oriental art objects.

BEACHY, P. A., residence, Oak Park, Ill.

DE RHODES, K. C., residence, South Bend, Ind.

FULLER, Grace, residence, Glencoe, Ill.

GRIDLEY, A. W., residence, Batavia, Ill.

HOYT, P. D., residence, Geneva, Ill.

MILLARD, George Madison, residence, Highland Park, Ill.

NICHOLAS, Frederick, residence, Flossmoor, Ill.

PETTIT MORTUARY CHAPEL, Belvedere, Ill.

RIVER FOREST TENNIS CLUB, River Forest, Ill.

SHAW, C. Thaxter, remodelling, Montreal, Que., Canada

Bock, Richard, studio-residence, Maywood, Ill.

Devin, Mrs. David, residence, Eliot, Me.

"A Fireproof House for $5,000," published in *Ladies Home Journal*

Gerts, Walter, residence, Glencoe, Ill.

Ludington, R. S., residence, Dwight, Ill.

Shaw, C. Thaxter, residence, Montreal, Que., Canada

Stone, Elizabeth, residence, Glencoe, Ill.

1907

Exhibition at Chicago Architectural Club.

BLOSSOM, George, garage addition, Chicago, Ill.

COONLEY, Avery, residence, Riverside, Ill. (The "Zoned" Prairie House—each function of the household in its own separate wing; v. Johnson, 1937.)

CUMMINGS, E. W., real estate office, River Forest, Ill.

FABYAN, Col. George, remodelling, Geneva, Ill.

FOX RIVER COUNTRY CLUB, remodelling, Geneva, Ill.

HUNT, Stephen E. B., residence, La Grange, Ill.

JAMESTOWN EXPOSITION PAVILION, for Larkin Co., Jamestown, Va.

MARTIN, Emma, (Fricke residence), alterations, Oak Park, Ill.

PEBBLES & BALCH, shop, Oak Park, Ill.

PORTER, Andrew T., "Tan-y-deri," residence, Spring Green, Wisc.

SUTTON, Harvey P., residence, McCook, Neb.

TOMEK, F. F., residence, Riverside, Ill.

WESTCOTT, Burton J., residence, Springfield, Ohio

McCormick, Harold, residence, Lake Forest, Ill.

Municipal Art Gallery, for Sherman Booth, Chicago, Ill.

Porter, Andrew T., residence (scheme #2), Spring Green, Wisc.

1908

The German philosopher Kuno Francke, visiting America, came to Oak Park to meet F.Ll.W. and see his work. The Wasmuth portfolio was to be the outcome of this meeting (v. 1910).

BOYNTON, E. E., residence, Rochester, N. Y.

BROWNE'S BOOKSTORE, Chicago, Ill.

DAVIDSON, Walter V., residence, Buffalo, N. Y.

EVANS, Robert W., residence, Chicago, Ill.

GILMORE, E. A., residence, Madison, Wisc.

HORNER, L. K., residence, Chicago, Ill.

LITTLE, Francis W., residence, Wayzata, Minn.

MAY, Meyer, residence, Grand Rapids, Mich.

ROBERTS, Isabel, residence, River Forest, Ill.

ROBIE, Frederick G., residence, Chicago, Ill.

STOCKMAN, Dr. G. C., residence, Mason City, Iowa

Baker, Frank J., residence (scheme #1), Wilmette, Ill.

Brigham, E. D., stables

Guthrie, William Norman, residence, Sewanee, Tenn.

Horseshoe Inn, for Willard Ashton, Estes Park, Colo.

Melson, J. G., residence, Mason City, Iowa

1909

F.Ll.W. closed studio, separated from family in Oak Park and went to Europe accompanied by Mamah Borthwick Cheney. Architect Von Holst remained in Oak Park to complete projects in working and construction stage.

ARCADE BUILDING, for Peter C. Stohr, Chicago, Ill.

BAKER, Frank J., residence (scheme #2), Wilmette, Ill.

CITY NATIONAL BANK AND HOTEL, for Blythe & Markley, Mason City, Iowa

CLARKE, Robert D., additions to Francis W. Little house, Peoria, Ill.

COPELAND, Dr. W. H., alterations, Oak Park, Ill.

INGALLS, J. Kibben, residence, River Forest, Ill.

STEFFENS, Oscar, residence, Chicago, Ill.

STEWART, George C., residence, Montecito, Calif.

THURBER, W. Scott, art gallery, Chicago, Ill.

ZIEGLER, Rev. J. R., residence, Frankfort, Ky.

Brown, Harry E., residence, Geneva, Ill.

City Dwelling with Glass Front, study

Larwell, residence, Muskegon, Mich.

Lexington Terrace, revision, for Edward C. Waller, Chicago, Ill.

Parker, Lawton, studio remodelling

Roberts, Mrs. Mary, residence, River Forest, Ill.

Town Hall, for Sherman Booth, Glencoe, Ill.

Town of Bitter Root, for Bitter Root Irrigation Co., Darby, Mont. (v. 1910)

Waller, Edward C., bathing pavilion, Charlevoix, Mich.

Waller, Edward C., small rental houses (three), River Forest, Ill.

1910

Visited Berlin, then took up residence in Fiesole, Italy, to prepare the drawings and text for the Wasmuth portfolio, first great monograph: *Ausgefuhrte Bauten Und Entwuerfe*, Berlin, 1910.

AMBERG, J. H., residence, Grand Rapids, Mich.

BLYTHE & MARKLEY, remodelling for law office, Chicago, Ill.

COMO ORCHARD SUMMER COLONY, for Como Orchard Land Co. (partly executed), Darby, Mont.

IRVING, E. P., residence, Decatur, Ill.

UNIVERSAL PORTLAND CEMENT CO., exhibit, Madison Square Garden, New York, N. Y.

Wright, Frank Lloyd, residence-studio, Viale Verdi, Fiesole, Italy (v. Sottil, 1957)

1911

Returned from Europe, built house and studio, "Taliesin," on ancestral farm lands near Spring Green, Wisc.

AMERICAN SYSTEM READY-CUT HOUSES, for Richards Co., Milwaukee, Wisc. (Some of the thirty-eight different designs for these pre-fabricated houses were constructed from shop plans.)

ANGSTER, Herbert C., residence, Lake Bluff, Ill.

BALCH, O. B., residence, Oak Park, Ill.

BANFF NATIONAL PARK PAVILION, Banff, Alb., Canada

BOOTH, Sherman, residence, Glencoe, Ill.

COONLEY, Avery, gardener's cottage, Riverside, Ill.

LAKE GENEVA INN, for Arthur L. Richards, Lake Geneva, Wisc.

WRIGHT, Frank Lloyd, "Taliesin," Spring Green, Wisc. (First use of stratified limestone wherein the wall and stone masses reiterate, in an abstract sense, the manner in which the native stone is found in the quarry; v. 1914, 1925.)

Adams, Harry S., residence, (scheme #1), Oak Park, Ill.

Booth, Sherman M., summer cottage

Christian Catholic Church, Zion, Ill.

Coonley, Avery, greenhouse, Riverside, Ill.

Coonley, Avery, kindergarten, Riverside, Ill.

Cutten, A. M., residence, Downer's Grove, Ill.

Esbenshade, E., residence, Milwaukee, Wisc.

Gerts, Walter, alterations, River Forest, Ill.

Heath, W. R., garage and stables, Buffalo, N. Y.

Madison Hotel, for Arthur L. Richards, Madison, Wisc.

North Shore Electric Waiting Station, for Sherman Booth, suburban Chicago, Ill.

Porter, Andrew T., residence (scheme #3), Spring Green, Wisc.

Schroeder, Edward, residence, Milwaukee, Wisc.

Wright, Frank Lloyd, residence, Chicago, Ill.

1912

Opened architectural office in Orchestra Hall, Chicago, Ill. Wrote and published *The Japanese Print: An Interpretation*, Seymour, Chicago, 1912.

COONLEY, Avery, playhouse, Riverside, Ill.

GREENE, William B., residence, Aurora, Ill.

PARK RIDGE COUNTRY CLUB, addition and alterations, Park Ridge, Ill.

Dress Shop, Oak Park, Ill.

Florida House, for Palm Beach, Fla.

Kehl Dance Academy, residence, shops, Madison, Wisc.

Press Building (San Francisco Call), for Spreckels Real Estate Co., San Francisco, Calif. (An early example of vertical articulation in a skyscraper.)

Schoolhouse, La Grange, Ill.

Small Town House

Taliesin Cottages (two), Spring Green, Wisc.

1913

ADAMS, Harry S., residence (scheme #2), Oak Park, Ill.

LITTLE, Francis W., residence (scheme #2), Wayzata, Minn.

MIDWAY GARDENS, Chicago, Ill. (Including designs for sculptured figures and murals. A remarkable instance of the allied arts of painting, sculpture and fresco worked into a harmonious whole by the architect.)

Block of City Row Houses, for Edward C. Waller, Chicago, Ill.

Carnegie Library, Ottawa, Ont., Canada

Hilly, M. B., residence, Brookfield, Ill.

Kellogg, J. W., residence, Milwaukee, Wisc.

Mendelsohn, Jerome, residence, Albany, N.Y.

1914

In August, an insane servant killed Mrs. Cheney and six others, then set fire to Taliesin and destroyed the house.

Aline Barnsdall visited F.Ll.W. to see about a theater design for Los Angeles (sketch made in 1914, developed in 1920).

Imperial Hotel Commission came to Taliesin to secure F.Ll.W. as the Emperor's architect for a new hotel in Tokyo. Before leaving for Japan, preliminary sketches were made.

Met Miriam Noel.

MORI, S. H., Oriental Art Studio, Chicago, Ill.

WRIGHT, Frank Lloyd, "Taliesin II," Spring Green, Wisc.

Concert Gardens, "Garden Project," Chicago, Ill.

Imperial Hotel, Tokyo, Japan. (Structural principle of the cantilever employed to give stability and flexibility when threatened by earthquakes; v. 1923.) (scheme #1; v. 1915.)

Jackson, Honoré J., three residences

State Bank, Spring Green, Wisc. (v. 1894)

United States Embassy, Tokyo, Japan

Vogelsang, John, dinner gardens and residence, Chicago, Ill.

1915

F.Ll.W. sailed to Japan acompanied by Miriam Noel (his second wife). Established residence and office in Tokyo in conjunction with work on the new Imperial Hotel. Under commission from William and John Spaulding, compiled the famed Spaulding Collection of Japanese Prints, now at the Museum of Fine Arts in Boston, Mass. At the same time, the architect's own collection of color prints, screens, bronzes and porcelains was increasing. The Emperor's art connoisseur, Hiromische Shugio, became a good friend of F.Ll.W. and guided his selection of Japanese works of art.

BACH, Emil, residence, Chicago, Ill.

BRIGHAM, E. D., residence, Glencoe, Ill.

GERMAN, A. D., warehouse, Richland Center, Wisc.

IMPERIAL HOTEL, revised scheme, including all tableware, carpets and furniture, Tokyo, Japan

RAVINE BLUFFS BRIDGE, for Sherman Booth, Glencoe, Ill.

RAVINE BLUFFS HOUSING DEVELOPMENT, for Sherman Booth, Glencoe, Ill.

Chinese Hospital, for the Rockefeller Foundation

Chinese Restaurant, for Arthur L. Richards, Milwaukee, Wisc.

A Lake Shore Residence

Model Quarter-Section Development, Chicago, Ill.

Wood, residence, Decatur, Ill.

1916

While working on Imperial Hotel, made several trips back to United States for work going on in Los Angeles office for Aline Barnsdall.

BAGLEY, Joseph J., residence, Grand Beach, Mich.

BARNSDALL, Aline, "Hollyhock House," residence, Los Angeles, Calif.

BOGK, F. C., residence, Milwaukee, Wisc.

CARR, W. S., residence, Grand Beach, Mich.

DUPLEX APARTMENTS, for Arthur Munkwitz, Milwaukee, Wisc. (Built from American System Ready-Cut, v. 1911.)

DUPLEX APARTMENTS, for Arthur L. Richards, Milwaukee, Wisc. (Built from American System Ready-Cut, v. 1911.)

IMPERIAL HOTEL ANNEX, Tokyo, Japan. (Temporary remodelling of existing building during construction of new hotel.)

VOSBURGH, Ernest, residence, Grand Beach, Mich.

Behn, residence, Grand Beach, Mich.

Converse, Clarence, residence, Palisades Park, Mich.

White, William Allen, remodelling, Emporia, Kans.

1917

The Imperial Hotel was mainly the property of the Emperor. Baron Okura was appointed the Emperor's representative to the architect and became a close friend and staunch supporter.

ALLEN, Henry J., residence, Wichita, Kans.

HUNT, Stephen M. B., residence, Oshkosh, Wisc.

HAYASHI, Aizaku, residence, Tokyo, Japan

Odawara Hotel, Nagoya, Japan

Powell, William, residence, Wichita, Kans.

1918

F.Ll.W. went to Peiping, China, to supervise weaving of his specially designed rugs for the Imperial Hotel. Visited famous monuments and art treasures of China as guest of Dr. Ku Hung Ming, noted Chinese writer and secretary to the Empress Dowager.

FUKUHARA, residence, Hakone, Japan

YAMAMURA, residence, Ashiya, Japan

Immu, Count, residence, Tokyo, Japan

Inouye, Viscount, residence, Tokyo, Japan

Motion Picture Theatre, Tokyo, Japan

1919

First Citation: Kenchiko Ho: Royal Household, Japan. Conferred by the Imperial Household, represented by Baron Okura.

Gallery for Japanese Prints, for William Spaulding, Boston, Mass.

Monolith Homes, for Thomas Hardy, Racine, Wisc.

1920

F.Ll.W.'s mother journeyed to Japan to visit him and was entertained by the Imperial Family, a rare circumstance for a Westerner in a nation where the Royal Household was carefully secluded.

BARNSDALL, Aline, residences A and B, Los Angeles, Calif.

WEBER, W. J., residence

Cantilevered Skyscraper, Sketches (v. National Life Insurance Company, 1924, and St. Mark's Tower, 1929)

Theater, Shops, Apartments for Aline Barnsdall, Olive Hill, Los Angeles, Calif.

1921

With "La Miniatura," inaugurated system of concrete blocks reinforced with steel rods, called "textile block."

GALE, Mrs. Thomas H., residence, Whitehall, Mich.

GIYU GAKUEN, School of the Free Spirit, Tokyo, Japan

MILLARD, Mrs. George Madison, "La Miniatura," residence, Pasadena, Calif.

Doheny Ranch Development, near Los Angeles, Calif.

Glass and Copper Skyscraper, preliminary sketches (later developed as St. Mark's Tower; v. 1929)

Goto, Baron, residence, Tokyo, Japan

Study for Block House, Los Angeles, Calif.

1922

Continued work on concrete block houses in Los Angeles, Calif.

BARNSDALL, Aline, "Little Dipper" Kindergarten, Los Angeles, Calif.

FREEMAN, Samuel, residence (third textile block home), Los Angeles, Calif.

LOWE, G. P., residence, Eagle Rock, Calif.

STORER, Dr. John, residence (second textile block home), Los Angeles, Calif.

Johnson, A. M., Desert Compound and Shrine, Death Valley, Calif.

Merchandising Building, copper, concrete and glass, Los Angeles, Calif.

Sachse, "Desert Springs," residence, Mojave Desert, Calif.

Tahoe Summer Colony, several cottages and barges, Lake Tahoe, Calif.

1923

F.Ll.W.'s mother died February 9.

Earthquake demolished much of Tokyo. Imperial Hotel survived, totally undamaged.

Wrote and published *Experimenting With Human Lives,* Los Angeles Fine Art Society, 1923 (concerning the earthquake and the Imperial Hotel).

ENNIS, Charles, residence (fourth textile block home), Los Angeles, Calif.

MOORE, Nathan G., residence, rebuilt after fire, Oak Park, Ill.

Martin, Darwin D., residence for daughter, Buffalo, N.Y.

1924

Separated from Miriam Noel Wright.

Louis H. Sullivan gave collection of his drawings to F.Ll.W. (This collection has since been sold by Mrs.

Wright to the Avery Architectural Library at Columbia University.) Sullivan died April 14.

Met Olgivanna Lazovich, daughter of Montenegro's Chief Justice, granddaughter of Duke Marko Milanov. She became his third wife.

SCULPTURE, series of Indian figures, in conjunction with Nakoma Project, Madison, Wisc.

Gladney, Mrs. Samuel, residence, Fort Worth, Tex.

Nakoma Country Club, Winnebago Camping Ground Indian Memorial, Madison, Wisc.

National Life Insurance Co. Skyscraper, for A. M. Johnson, Chicago, Ill. (A development of cantilevered skyscraper scheme of 1920 in concrete, metal and glass.)

Planetarium and Automobile Objective, for Gordon Strong, Sugar Loaf Mountain, Maryland

1925

Taliesin burned for the second time. (In both fires at Taliesin, only the living quarters were destroyed. The studio, office, workshops and out-lying wings of the building were spared and remain today, with subsequent modifications and remodelling, much as they were when first constructed in 1911.)

Wendingen published by H. Th. Wijdeveld in Holland. Considered by F.Ll.W. to be the most beautiful monograph of his work.

WRIGHT, Frank Lloyd, "Taliesin III," Spring Green, Wisc.

Millard, Mrs. George Madison, gallery, Pasadena, Calif.

Phi Gamma Delta Fraternity House, Madison, Wisc.

Steel Cathedral, for William Norman Guthrie, New York, N.Y.

1926

Designed covers for *Liberty* magazine.

Daughter, Iovanna, born to Mr. and Mrs. Wright in Chicago. Adopted Svetlana, 7-year-old daughter of Mrs. Wright by previous marriage.

"Liberty" Magazine Covers (not used)

"Kinder Symphony," five playhouses for Oak Park (Ill.) Playgrounds

Skyscraper Regulation, Chicago, Ill.

Standardized Concrete & Copper Gas Station

1927

Honorary Member: Academie Royale des Beaux Arts, Belgium. Conferred by the state.

Began series of articles under the heading "In the Cause of Architecture," subsequently published monthly in *The Architectural Record.*

Shortly after the birth of Iovanna, Mr. and Mrs. Wright visited Puerto Rico. Later, in Minneapolis, Mrs. Wright urged her husband to begin his autobiography.

Albert McArthur asked Frank Lloyd Wright to help him with designs for Arizona Biltmore Hotel in Phoenix. Winter of 1927-28, Mr. and Mrs. Wright resided at 108 Almeria St., Phoenix, while working on Biltmore. At this time, Dr. Alexander Chandler of Chandler, Ariz., contacted F.Ll.W. regarding proposed scheme for desert hotel resort (v. 1928).

> ARIZONA BILTMORE (in association with Albert McArthur), for Warren McArthur, Phoenix, Ariz.
>
> MARTIN, Darwin D., residence, Derby, N.Y.

1928

While living in La Jolla, Calif., F.Ll.W. drew preliminary sketches for Dr. Alexander Chandler Project. Upon returning to the desert, he spent the winter of 1928-29 at "Ocatillo," his Southwestern Headquarters built near the site of the proposed San Marcos-in-the-Desert. This camp was F.Ll.W.'s first use of textiles in architecture; canvas-topped, box-board cabins formed an enclosed compound on a small desert hill. Later, this theme of textiles in architecture was adapted for the San Marcos Water Gardens; then again, on a much larger scale, at Taliesin West (v. 1938).

> WRIGHT, Frank Lloyd, "Ocatillo," Southwestern headquarters, Chandler, Ariz.
>
> *Beach Cottages,* Ras-El-Bar Island, Damiette, Egypt
>
> *Blue Sky Burial Terraces,* for Darwin D. Martin, Buffalo, N.Y.
>
> *Cudney,* Wellington & Ralph, residence, Chandler, Ariz. (part of San Marcos-in-the-Desert)
>
> *Jones,* Richard Lloyd (scheme #1), Tulsa, Okla.
>
> *Low-Cost Concrete Block Houses,* Chandler, Ariz.
>
> *San Marcos-In-The-Desert,* resort hotel for Dr. Alexander Chandler, Chandler, Ariz.
>
> *San Marcos Hotel,* alterations, Chandler, Ariz.
>
> *San Marcos Water Gardens,* Chandler, Ariz. (An innovation of the highway motel.)
>
> *School for Negro Children,* for the Rosenwald Foundation, La Jolla, Calif.
>
> *Simple Block House* for Chandler, Ariz.
>
> *Young,* Owen D., residence, Chandler, Ariz. (part of San Marcos-in-the-Desert)

1929

Extraordinary Honorary Member: Akademie der Kunst (Royal Academy), Berlin. Conferred by the Reich.

Left Arizona in May, returned to Wisconsin, then to New York City to discuss plans for St. Mark's Tower with William Norman Guthrie.

Continued to work on projects for Chandler, but following the stock market crash on October 29, these projects came to a halt.

> JONES, Richard Lloyd, residence (scheme #2), Tulsa, Okla.
>
> *St. Mark's Tower,* for William Norman Guthrie, New York, N.Y.

1930

Delivered famous Kahn Lectures at Princeton, published under title *Modern Architecture,* Princeton University Press, 1930.

Continued work on autobiography with Mrs. Wright, and *The Disappearing City.*

> LEERDAM GLASS, Holland; vases and glassware
>
> *Automobile Design,* with cantilevered top
>
> *Cabins for Desert or Woods,* for Chicago YMCA
>
> *Designs for Tableware* (nine)
>
> *Grouped Apartment Towers* (based on St. Mark's Tower), Chicago, Ill.
>
> *Noble,* Elizabeth, apartment house, Los Angeles, Calif.

1931

Mr. and Mrs. Wright visited Rio de Janeiro as guests of Pan American Union to judge a series of designs for the Columbus Memorial.

Exhibition of life work to New York City; Amsterdam; Berlin; Frankfurt; Stuttgart; Belgium; Milwaukee, Wisc.; Eugene, Ore.; Chicago, Ill.

> *Capital Journal Building,* Salem, Ore.
>
> *"House On the Mesa,"* for Denver, Colo.
>
> *Three Schemes for "A Century of Progress,"* 1933 Chicago World's Fair, Chicago, Ill.

1932

Mr. and Mrs. Wright founded the Taliesin Fellowship, the pioneering venture in architectural education that continues now as The Frank Lloyd Wright School of Architecture. Hillside Home School buildings (v. 1902) were left by the Lloyd Jones aunts to F.Ll.W., and were converted to the Taliesin Fellowship complex (v. 1933).

An Autobiography published by Longmans Green. *The Disappearing City* published by William Farquhar Payson. The ideas published in this book on decentralization finally began to take root in America 30 years later. While working on this book, F.Ll.W. formed his concepts of Broadacre City; v. 1933.

Honorary Member: National Academy of Brazil.

> *Automobile and Airplane Filling and Service Stations*
>
> *Cinema and Shops* (John Lloyd Wright Associates), Michigan City, Ind.

Conventional House, block-shell, copper and glass
Farm Units, prefabricated sheet steel
Highway Overpass Design
"Life House"
New Theater
Norm of the Pre-Fabricated House
Overhead Filling Station
Roadside Markets, prefabricated sheet steel and glass
Willey, Dean Malcolm M., residence (scheme #1), Minneapolis, Minn.

1933

First year of annual move to Arizona with entire Taliesin Fellowship. Spent at Chandler, Ariz. Began work on actual model of Broadacre City, incorporating many new as well as previous schemes for decentralized living.

HILLSIDE THEATER CURTAIN

TALIESIN FELLOWSHIP COMPLEX, Spring Green, Wisc. (Executed in part. Large drafting room added to the existing Hillside Home School building; original gymnasium transformed into theater-playhouse; extensive remodelling for new dining room, kitchen, apprentices' rooms, galleries, and exhibition rooms.)

1934

Continued work on Broadacre City. Development of separate projects and completion of entire model. Exhibited in United States.

BROADACRE CITY MODEL, illustrating the program outlined in *The Disappearing City*

PLAN FOR PRESENTATION OF BROADACRE CITY EXHIBIT, including model stands and general layout

WILLEY, Dean Malcolm E., residence (scheme #2), Minneapolis, Minn.

Heliocopter
Road Machine (motor car)
Train
Zoned House No. 1

1935

Edgar S. Kaufmann, Sr., exhibited Broadacre City the previous year in Pittsburgh, then commissioned F.Ll.W. to design his home, "Fallingwater."

KAUFMANN, Edgar J., Sr., "Fallingwater," residence, Bear Run, Pa.

Hoult, H. C., residence (the first Usonian House), Wichita, Kans.

Lusk, Robert D., residence, Huron, S. Dak.

Marcus, Stanley, residence, Dallas, Tex.
Zoned House, city version
Zoned House, country version
Zoned House, suburban version

1936

The administration building of the Johnson's Wax company was another great pioneer in architecture. The dendriform columns completely eliminated post and beam construction, bringing a new plasticity into architecture and engineering.

Based on the Hoult house of 1935, the Jacobs house was the first constructed low-cost home with floor heating and shop-fabricated walls. Called by F.Ll.W. "The Usonian House."

For Paul Hanna, F.Ll.W. designed a home based on the hexagon (honey-comb) unit system for more flexibility of plan—a natural step from the square to the circle.

HANNA, Paul R., residence, Palo Alto, Calif.

JACOBS, Herbert, residence, Westmoreland, Wisc.

JOHNSON, S. C. & SON, INC., administration building, Racine, Wisc.

ROBERTS, Mrs. Abby Beecher, residence, Marquette, Mich.

Chandler, Dr. Alexander, hotel remodelling, Chandler, Ariz.

Little San Marcos-In-The-Desert, resort inn for Dr. Alexander Chandler, Chandler, Ariz.

1937

Invited to travel to Russia with Mrs. Wright as guests of the Soviet Union, in order to attend World Conference of Architects.

Wrote and published (with Baker Brownell) *Architecture and Modern Life,* Harper, 1937.

Developed a system of all-steel houses for Los Angeles, employing industrial products and techniques, for housing.

JOHNSON, Herbert F., "Wingspread," residence, Racine, Wisc. (Called by F.Ll.W. "The Last Prairie House," a zoned plan development of the Coonley House; v. 1908.)

KAUFMANN, Edgar J., Sr., office, Pittsburgh, Pa.

"All-Steel" Houses, development of one hundred, Los Angeles, Calif.

Borglum, Gutson, studio, Black Hills, S. Dak.

Bramson, Leo, dress shop, Oak Park, Ill.

Memorial to the Soil, chapel in cast concrete, for southern Wisc.

Notz, Hulda and Louise, residence, Pittsburgh, Pa.

Parker, George, garage, Janesville, Wisc.

1938

Commissioned by Dr. Ludd Spivey to design a new campus for Florida Southern College in Lakeland. Construction continued over a period of twenty years.

FLORIDA SOUTHERN COLLEGE, Lakeland, Fla.

KAUFMANN, Edgar J., Sr., guest house addition to "Fallingwater," Bear Run, Pa.

MIDWAY FARM BUILDINGS, Taliesin, Spring Green, Wisc.

REBHUHN, Ben, residence, Great Neck, N.Y.

TALIESIN WEST, Frank Lloyd Wright Foundation Winter Headquarters, Scottsdale, Ariz. (Construction continues, following a master plan set down by the architect and being executed under Mrs. Wright's supervision.)

"House For A Family of $5,000-$6,000 Income," for *Life* magazine.

Jester, Ralph, residence, Palos Verdes, Calif. (Curved plywood walls; an all plywood house.)

Johnson, Herbert F., Jr., gatehouse, farm group, Wind Point, north of Racine, Wisc.

Jurgensen, Royal H., residence, Evanston, Ill.

McCallum, George Bliss, residence, Northampton, Mass.

Monona Terrace, Madison Civic Center, Madison, Wisc.

Smith, E. A., "Pinetree House," residence, Piedmont Pines, Calif.

1939

Invited to London to deliver a series of lectures at The Sulgrave Manor Board, later published as *An Organic Architecture,* Lund Humphries, London, 1939.

Honorary Degree: Master of Arts, conferred by Wesleyan University.

ARMSTRONG, Andrew F. H., residence, near Gary, Ind.

GOETSCH-WINKLER, residence (scheme #1), Okemos, Mich.

ROSENBAUM, Stanley, residence, Florence, Ala.

SCHWARTZ, Bernard, residence, Two Rivers, Wisc.

STURGES, George D., residence, Brentwood Heights, Calif.

"SUNTOP HOMES," quadruple house, Ardmore, Pa.

Bell, Lewis N., residence, Los Angeles, Calif.

Carlson, Edith, residence, Superior, Wisc.

Crystal Heights Hotel, Shops, Theaters, Washington, D.C.

Front Gates, Taliesin, Spring Green, Wisc.

Lowenstein, Gordon, residence, Mason City, Iowa

Mauer, Edgar A., residence, Los Angeles, Calif.

Spivey, Dr. Ludd M., residence, Fort Lauderdale, Fla.

Usonian House Development of seven buildings, Okemos, Mich. Goetsch-Winkler (built on different site), Brauner, Garrison, Hause, Newman, Panshin, Van Duesen.

1940

Exhibition at the Museum of Modern Art, New York, N.Y.

BAIRD, Theodore, residence, Amherst, Mass.

BAZETT, Sidney, residence, Hillsborough, Calif.

CHRISTIE, James B., residence, Bernardsville, N.J.

COMMUNITY CHURCH, Kansas City, Mo.

EUCHTMAN, Joseph, residence, Baltimore, Md.

LEWIS, Lloyd, residence, Libertyville, Ill.

MANSON, Charles L., residence, Wausau, Wisc.

PAUSON, Rose, residence, Phoenix, Ariz.

PEW, John C., residence, Madison, Wisc.

POPE, Loren, residence, Falls Church, Va.

SONDERN, Clarence, residence, Kansas City, Mo.

STEVENS, Leigh, "Auldbrass," plantation, near Yemassee, S.C.

Model House—Museum of Modern Art, New York, N.Y.

Nesbitt, John, residence, Carmel Bay, Calif.

Oboler, Arch, "Eaglefeather," residence (scheme #1), Los Angeles, Calif.

Pence, Martin J., residence, Hilo, Hawaii

Rentz, Frank A., residence, Madison, Wisc.

Watkins, Franklin, studio, Barnegat City, N.J.

Methodist Church, Spring Green, Wisc.

1941

Honorary Member: The Royal Institute of British Architects. Conferred by King George VI.

The Sir George Watson Chair: Royal Institute of British Architects. Academic honor by The Sulgrave Manor Board.

The Royal Gold Medal for Architecture. The Royal Institute of British Architects. Conferred by King George VI.

AFFLECK, Gregor, residence, Bloomfield Hills, Mich.

GRIGGS, Chauncey, residence, Tacoma, Wash.

OBOLER, Arch, gate house, retreat, Los Angeles, Calif.

RICHARDSON, Stuart, residence, Glenridge, N. J.

WALL, Carlton David, "Snowflake," residence, Plymouth, Mich.

Barton, John, residence, Pine Bluff, Wisc.

Dayer, Walter, music studio, Detroit, Mich. (v. 1946)

Ellinwood, Alfred H., residence, Deerfield, Ill.

Field, Parker B., residence, Peru, Ill.

Guenther, William, "Mountain Lakes," residence, East Caldwell, N. J.

Petersen, Roy, residence, West Racine, Wisc.
Schevill, Margaret, residence, Tuscon, Ariz.
Sigma Chi Fraternity House, Hanover, Ind.
Sundt, Vigo, residence, Madison, Wisc.
Waterstreet, Mary, studio, near Spring Green, Wisc.

1942

Honorary Member: National Academy of Architects, Uruguay.

ALTERATIONS TO LINCOLN CONTINENTAL owned by F.Ll.W.

JACOBS, Herbert, "Solar Hemicycle" house, residence, Middleton, Wisc.

Burlingham, Lloyd, residence, El Paso, Tex.

Circle Pines Center, Cloverdale, Mich.

Cloverleaf Quadruple Housing, for U. S. Government, Pittsfield, Mass.

Cooperative Homesteads, berm-type low-cost housing project for Detroit Auto Workers, Detroit, Mich.

Foreman, Clark, residence, Washington, D. C.

1943

Published revised edition of *An Autobiography,* Duell, Sloan and Pearce, 1943.

Honorary Member: National Academy of Architects of Mexico. Conferred by the state.

Solomon R. Guggenheim commissioned Frank Lloyd Wright to design a museum for his collection of non-objective paintings. For the first time in architecture one continuous spiral ramp, encircling an open court, gives total plasticity in vertical movement. First sketches made in 1943; construction begun in 1956. The completed building was dedicated by Mrs. Frank Lloyd Wright shortly after the architect's death in 1959.

GUGGENHEIM MUSEUM, for Solomon R. Guggenheim, New York, N. Y.

Hein, M. N., residence, Chippewa Falls, Wisc.

McDonald, T. L., residence, Washington, D. C.

Restaurant and Service Station, for Glen Richardson, Spring Green, Wisc.

1944

The S.C. Johnson & Son, Co. again asked F.Ll.W. for a design, this time for a research tower. He conceived it in alternating levels of square floors and round balconies, all cantilevered from a central core which contains utilities and elevators. Glass tubing encloses the interior, providing soft, diffused lighting within.

JOHNSON, S.C. & SONS, INC., research tower, Racine, Wisc.

Loeb, Gerald M., "Pergola House," residence, Redding, Conn.

Harlan, P. K., residence, Omaha, Neb.

Wells, Stuart, residence, Minneapolis, Minn.

1945

Wrote *When Democracy Builds,* University of Chicago Press, 1945, a revision of *The Disappearing City,* incorporating Broadacre City model and plans.

FRIEDMAN, Arnold, residence, Pecos, New M.

GRANT, Douglas, residence, Cedar Rapids, Iowa

TALIESIN DAMS, Spring Green, Wisc.

Adelman Laundry, for Benjamin Adelman and Sons, Milwaukee, Wisc.

Berdan, George, residence, Ludington, Mich.

Desert Spa, for Elizabeth Arden, Phoenix, Ariz.

"*Glass House,*" for *Ladies Home Journal*

Haldorn, Stuart, "The Wave," residence, Carmel, Calif.

Slater, William R., residence, Rhode Island

Stamm, residence, Lake Delavan, Wisc.

1946

Honorary Member: The National Academy of Finland. Conferred by the state.

BRAUNER, Erling P., residence (Usonia II), Okemos, Mich.

WALTER, Lowell, residence and river pavilion, Quasqueton, Iowa

Dana, Malcolm, President's House, residence, Olivet College, Olivet, Mich.

Dayer, Walter, residence and music pavilion (scheme #2), Bloomfield Hills, Mich.

Garrison, J. J., residence (Usonia I), Lansing, Mich.

Hause, C. O., residence, Lansing, Mich.

Housing, for State Teachers College, Lansing, Mich.

Morris, V. C., residence (scheme #1), San Francisco, Calif.

Munroe, Joe, residence, Knox County, Ohio

Newman, residence (Usonia I), Lansing, Mich.

Oboler, Arch, studio, Los Angeles, Calif.

Panshin, Alexis, residence, State Teachers College, Lansing, Mich.

Pinderton, William, residence, Cambridge, Mass.

Pinkerton, W. M., residence, Fairfax County, Va.

Rogers Lacy Hotel, Dallas, Tex.

Sarabhi Administration Building and Store, Amedabad, India

Van Dusen, residence (Usonia I), Lansing, Mich.

1947

Honorary Degree: Doctor of Fine Arts, Princeton University. A year of many revolutionary designs, including the Unitarian Church based on the triangle—symbol of aspiration—with its sheltering roof formed as two hands in prayer, and the Huntington Hartford, Pittsburgh Point and Butterfly Bridge projects, showing advanced engineering principles molded into great architectural forms.

ALPAUGH, Amy, residence, Northport, Mich.

BULBULLIAN, Dr. A. H., residence, Rochester, Minn.

GALESBURG VILLAGE DWELLINGS: MASTER PLAN, Kalamazoo, Mich.

KAUFMANN, Edgar J., Sr., guest house alterations, Bear Run, Pa.

KEYS, Thomas E., residence (two schemes, second built), Rochester, Minn.

LAMBERSON, Jack, residence, Oskaloosa, Iowa

MEETING HOUSE FOR THE FIRST UNITARIAN SOCIETY, Madison, Wisc.

PARKWYN VILLAGE DWELLINGS: MASTER PLAN, Kalamazoo, Mich.

USONIA HOMES: MASTER PLAN, Pleasantville, N. Y.

Auto Display Room and Workshop, for Roy Wetmore, Detroit, Mich.

Bell, Dr. Charles, residence, E. St. Louis, Ill.

Black, B. Marden, residence, Rochester, Minn.

Boomer, Jorgine, residence, Phoenix, Ariz. (v. Pauson, 1940)

Butterfly Bridge, for Wisconsin River, Spring Green, Wisc.

Cottage Group Resort Hotel, for Huntington Hartford, Hollywood, Calif.

Depot, for San Antonio Transit Co., San Antonio, Tex.

Funeral Chapels, for Nicholas P. Daphne, San Francisco, Calif.

Grieco, Vito, residence, Andover, Mass.

Hamilton, Berta, residence, Brookline, Vt.

Hartford, Huntington, residence, Hollywood, Calif.

Houston, Walter S., Schuyler County, Ill.

Keith, R. H., residence, Oakland County, Mich.

Marting, E. L., residence, Northampton, Ohio

Palmer, Dr. Paul V., residence, Phoenix, Ariz.

Pike, John J., residence, Los Angeles, Calif.

Pittsburgh Point Park, community and civic center (scheme #1; v. 1948), Pittsburgh, Pa.

Rand, Ayn, residence, near Redding, Conn.

Sports Club, for Huntington Hartford, Hollywood, Calif.

Wheeler, Frank G., residence, Hinsdale, Ill.

Wilkie, Donald, residence, Hennepin County, Minn.

Valley National Bank, Tucson, Ariz.

1948

Began to write about his life and work with Louis H. Sullivan (v. 1949).

ADELMAN, Albert, residence, Fox Point, Wisc.

ALSOP, Carroll, residence, Oskaloosa, Iowa

ANTHONY, Howard, residence, Benton Harbor, Mich.

BUEHLER, Maynard P., residence, Orinda, Calif.

EPPSTEIN, Samuel, residence, Galesburg Village, Kalamazoo, Mich.

GREINER, Ward, residence, Parkwyn Village, Kalamazoo, Mich.

HUGHES, J. Willis, "Fountainhead," residence, Jackson, Miss.

LAURENT, Kenneth, residence, Rockford, Ill.

LEVIN, Robert, residence, Parkwyn Village, Kalamazoo, Mich.

MOSSBERG, Herman T., residence, South Bend, Ind.

PRATT, Eric, residence, Galesburg Village, Kalamazoo, Mich.

ROSENBAUM, Stanley, addition to residence, Florence, Ala.

SMITH, Melvyn Maxwell, residence, Bloomfield Hills, Mich.

V.C. MORRIS SHOP, for V.C. Morris, San Francisco, Calif.

WALKER, Mrs. Clinton, residence, Carmel, Calif.

WELTZIEMER, C. E., residence, Oberlin, Ohio

Adelman, Benjamin, residence, Fox Point, Wisc.

Barney, Maginel Wright, cottage, Spring Green, Wisc.

Bergman, Alfred, residence, St. Petersburg, Fla.

Bimson, Walter, penthouse, Phoenix, Ariz.

Crater Resort, Meteor Crater, Ariz.

Daphne, Nicholas, residence, San Francisco, Calif.

Ellison, Henry, residence, Bridgewater Township, N. J.

Feenberg, Ben, residence, Fox Point, Wisc.

Hageman, George, residence, Peoria, Ill.

Margolis, Dr. Frederick, residence, Kalamazoo, Mich.

McCord, Glenn, residence, N. Arlington, N. J.

Miller, Sidney, residence, Pleasantville, N. Y.

Muehlberger, C. W., residence, E. Lansing, Mich.

Pittsburgh Point Park, community and civic center (scheme #2), Pittsburgh, Pa.

Prout, George M., residence, Columbus, Ind.

Scully, Vincent, residence, Woodbridge, Conn.

Smith, Talbot, residence, Ann Arbor, Mich.

Valley National Bank and Shopping Center, Sunny-slope, Ariz.

1949

Published book on Louis H. Sullivan, *Genius and the Mobocracy*, Duell, Sloan & Pearce, 1949.

Honorary Member: The American National Institute of Arts and Letters.

The Gold Medal of the American Institute of Architects. Conferred by the Institute.

The Gold Medal of the Philadelphia Chapter of the American Institute of Architects.

Honorary Degree: The Peter Cooper Award for the Advancement of Art.

ADLER, Arnold, additions to Sondern House, Kansas City, Mo.

CABARET-THEATER, Taliesin West, Scottsdale, Ariz.

EDWARDS, James, residence, Okemos, Mich.

FRIEDMAN, Sol, residence, Usonia Homes, Pleasant-ville, N. Y.

MC CARTNEY, Ward, residence, Parkwyn Village, Kalamazoo, Mich.

SERLIN, Ed, residence, Usonia Homes, Pleasantville, N. Y.

WEISBLATT, *David*, residence, Galesburg Village, Kalamazoo, Mich.

Bloomfield, L. A., residence, Tucson, Ariz.

Dabney, Charles, residence, near Chicago, Ill.

Drummond, Alan, residence, Santa Fe, New M.

Goetsch-Winkler, residence (scheme #2), Okemos, Mich.

Griswold, George, residence, Greenwich, Conn.

John, Harry G., residence, Oconomowoc, Wisc.

Lea, Thomas C., residence, Asheville, N. C.

Publicker, Robert, residence, Haverford, Pa.

San Francisco Bay Bridge, Southern Crossing, San Francisco, Calif.

Self-Service Garage, for Edgar J. Kaufmann, Pittsburgh, Pa.

Theater, for the New Theater Corporation, Hartford, Conn.

Windfohr, Robert, residence, Fort Worth, Tex.

YWCA Building, Racine, Wisc.

1950

Honorary Degree: Doctor of Laws, Florida Southern College.

Centennial Award: *Popular Mechanics* magazine.

ANDERTON COURT CENTER, Beverly Hills, Calif.

BERGER, Robert, residence, San Anselmo, Calif.

BROWN, Eric, residence, Parkwyn Village, Kalamazoo, Mich.

CARLSON, Raymond, residence, Phoenix, Ariz.

CARR, John O., residence, Glenview, Ill.

DAVIS, Dr. Richard, residence, Marion, Ind.

GILLIN, John, residence, Dallas, Tex.

HARPER, Dr. Ina Moriss, residence, St. Joseph, Mich.

MATHEWS, Arthur C., residence, Atherton, Calif.

MEYER, Curtis, residence, Galesburg Village, Kalamazoo, Mich.

MILLER, Drs. Alvin and Walter, residence, Charles City, Iowa

MUIRHEAD, Robert, residence, Plato Center, Ill.

NEILS, Henry J., residence, Minneapolis, Minn.

O'DONNELL, Dale, residence, E. Lansing, Mich.

PALMER, William, residence, Ann Arbor, Mich.

SCHABERG, Donald, residence (scheme #2), Okemos, Mich.

SHAVIN, Seymour, residence, Chattanooga, Tenn.

SMITH, Richard, residence, Jefferson, Wisc.

SWEETON, J. A., residence, Merchantville, N. J.

WINN, Robert D., residence, Parkwyn Village, Kalamazoo, Mich.

WRIGHT, David, residence, Phoenix, Ariz.

ZIMMERMAN, Isadore, residence, Manchester, N. H.

Achuff, Harold, residence, Wauwatosa, Wisc.

Auerbach, Irwin, residence, Pleasantville, N. Y.

Bush, Robert N., residence, Arkansas

Carroll, Thomas, residence, Wauwatosa, Wisc.

Chahroudi, A. K., residence (scheme #1), Lake Mahopac, N. Y.

Conklin, Tom D., residence, new Ulm, Minn.

Grover, Donald, residence, Syracuse, N. Y.

Hargrove, Kenneth, residence, Berkeley, Calif.

Jackson, Arnold, residence, Madison, Wisc.

Jacobsen, George, residence, Montreal, Que., Canada

Montooth, George, residence, Rushville, Ill.

Sabin, Brainerd, residence, Battle Creek, Mich.

Schaberg, Donald, residence (scheme #1), Okemos, Mich.

Small, Dr. Leon, residence, West Orange, N. J.

Southwestern Christian Seminary, for Dr. Peyton Canary, Phoenix, Ariz.

Stevens, Arthur J., residence, Park Ridge, Ill.

Strong, Lawrence, residence, Kalamazoo, Mich.

Wassel, William S., residence, Philadelphia, Pa.

1951

The "Usonian Automatic," designed in this year, was based on the concrete shell-block (steel-rod reinforced) system first devised thirty years earlier in California, but carried the idea further for new construction methods.

A vast exhibit, entitled "Sixty Years of Living Architecture," consisting of models, photographs and original drawings, began a world tour, opening in the Palazzo Strozzi, Florence. The de Medici Medal was conferred by the city of Florence and awarded in full ceremony at the Palazzo Vecchio. Star of Solidarity, one of Europe's most coveted and rarely conferred medals, was awarded to F.Ll.W. in the Doge's Palace, Venice, in a ceremony of medieval splendor.

ADELMAN, Benjamin, "Usonian Automatic," residence, Phoenix, Ariz.

AUSTIN, Misses Gabrielle and Charlcey, residence, Greenville, S. C.

CHAHROUDI, A. K., cottage (scheme #2), Lake Mahopac, N. Y.

ELAM, S. P., residence, Austin, Minn.

FULLER, W. L., residence, Pass Christian, Miss.

GLORE, Charles F., residence, Lake Forest, Ill.

JOHNSON, S. C. & SON, INC., office alterations, Racine, Wisc.

KINNEY, Patrick, residence, Lancaster, Wisc.

KRAUS, Russell, residence, Kirkwood, Mo.

PEARCE, Wilbur C., residence, Monrovia, Calif.

REISLEY, Roland, residence, Usonia Homes, Pleasantville, N. Y.

RUBIN, Nathan, residence, Canton, Ohio

STALEY, Karl A., residence, Madison, Ohio

Clarke, George, cottage, Carmel, Calif.

Hall, Louis B., residence, Ann Arbor, Mich.

Haynes, John P., residence, Fort Wayne, Ind.

Kaufmann, E. J., "Boulder House," residence, Palm Spring, Calif.

Schevill, Margaret, studio, Tucson, Ariz.

1952

Exhibit, "Sixty Years of Living Architecture," travelled from Florence to Zurich, Paris, Munich, Rotterdam.

During the summer, Harold C. Price, Sr. visited Taliesin to ask F.Ll.W. for a design of a small office building. Upon the architect's suggestion, he ventured into a 19-story skyscraper scheme that would house his own company's offices and offer further rental space and apartments. Founded upon the St. Mark's project of 1929.

BLAIR, Quentin, residence, Cody, Wyo.

BRANDES, Ray, residence, Bellevue, Wash.

GODDARD, Lewis H., residence, Plymouth, Mich.

HILLSIDE PLAYHOUSE (burned 1952), redesigned and rebuilt, Spring Green, Wisc.

HILLSIDE THEATER CURTAIN #2, Spring Green, Wisc.

LEWIS, George, residence, Tallahassee, Fla.

LINDHOLM, R. W., residence, Cloquet, Minn.

MARDEN, Luis, residence, McLean, Va.

PIEPER, Arthur, residence, Paradise Valley, Ariz.

PRICE TOWER, office and apartment building for H. C. Price Co., Bartlesville, Okla.

TEATER, Archie B., residence, Bliss, Idaho

Affleck, Gregor, residence (scheme #2), Bloomfield Hills, Mich.

Bailleres, Raoul, residence, Acapulco, Mexico

Clifton, William, residence, Oakland, N. J.

Cooke, Andrew B., residence, Virginia Beach, Va.

Leesburg Floating Gardens, Leesburg, Fla.

"Paradise on Wheels," trailer park for Lee Ackerman, Paradise Valley, Ariz.

Sturtevant, Lawrence, residence, Oakland, Calif.

Swan, Lawrence, residence, near Detroit, Mich.

Wainer, Alexis, residence, Valdosta, Ga.

Zeta Beta Tau Fraternity House, Gainesville, Fla.

1953

Exhibit, "Sixty Years of Living Architecture," crossed the Atlantic to Mexico City and New York, after two years in Europe.

Honorary Member: The Akademie Royale des Beaux Arts, Stockholm. Conferred by the state.

Honorary Member: The National Academy of Finland. Conferred by the state.

Published *The Future of Architecture*, Horizon Press, N. Y., 1953. (This is the first book published by Horizon Press for F.Ll.W., beginning a long and fruitful association between architect and publisher.)

BOOMER, Jorgine, cottage, Phoenix, Ariz.

DOBKINS, John J., residence, Canton, Ohio

PENFIELD, Louis, residence (scheme #1), Willoughby, Ohio

RIVERVIEW TERRACE, restaurant, Spring Green, Wisc.

SANDER, Frank S., residence, Stamford, Conn.

USONIAN EXHIBITION HOUSE, an exhibition pavilion, New York, N. Y.

WRIGHT, Robert Llewellyn, residence, Silver Springs, Md.

Brewer, Joseph, residence, E. Fishkill, N. Y.

Lee, Edgar S., residence, Midland, Mich.

Masieri Memorial Building, Grand Canal, Venice, Italy

Morris, V. C., "Seacliff," residence (scheme #2), San Francisco, Calif.

Pieper and *Montooth*, office building, Scottsdale, Ariz.

Point View Residences, two schemes for apartment towers for the Edgar J. Kaufmann Charitable Trust, Pittsburgh, Pa.

FM Radio Station, for William B. Proxmire, Jefferson, Wisc.

Rhododendron Chapel, for Edgar J. Kaufmann, Bear Run, Pa.

Yosemite National Park Restaurant, Calif.

1954

Exhibit, "Sixty Years of Living Architecture," went to Los Angeles, Calif., then returned to Taliesin.

Citation and Brown Medal: The Franklin Institute of Philadelphia. Conferred by the Institute. Honorary Degree: Doctor of Fine Arts, Yale University.

Wrote and published *The Natural House,* Horizon Press, 1954, an important work describing the moderate-cost home for America, including detailed drawings and explanations of the "Usonian Automatic."

BACHMAN-WILSON, A., residence, Millstone, N. J.

BETH SHOLOM SYNAGOGUE, Elkins Park, Pa. (A temple to Judaism, expressing its history and ritual in architectural form.)

BOULTER, Cedric, residence, Cincinnati, Ohio

CHRISTIAN, John, residence, Lafayette, Ind.

CLARKE-ARNOLD, residence, Columbus, Wisc.

EXHIBITION PAVILION, remodelling of wing of Hollyhock House, Olive Hill, Los Angeles, Calif.

FAWCETT, Randall, residence, Los Banos, Calif.

FEIMAN, Ellis, residence, Canton, Ohio

FREDERICK, Louis B., residence, Barrington, Ill.

GREENBERG, Dr. Maurice, residence, Dousman, Wisc.

HAGAN, I. N., residence, Uniontown, Pa.

KELAND, Willard, residence, Racine, Wisc.

PRICE, Harold C., Jr., residence, Bartlesville, Okla.

PRICE, Harold C., Sr., residence, Phoenix, Ariz.

THAXTON, William L., residence, Houston, Tex.

Barnsdall Park Municipal Gallery, City of Los Angeles, Calif.

Christian Science Reading Room, Riverside, Ill.

Clinic, for Dr. Alfons Tipshus, Stockton, Calif.

Cornwell, Gibbons, residence, West Goshen, Pa.

Department Store, Freund y Cia, San Salvador, El Salvador

Rebhuhn, Ben, residence, Fort Meyers, Fla.

Schwenn, Roger, residence, Verona, Wisc.

1955

Honorary Degree: Doctor of Fine Arts, University of Wisconsin.

Honorary Degree: The Technische Hochschule of Darmstadt, Germany. Conferred by the nation.

Honorary Degree: The Technische Hochschule of Zurich, Switzerland. Conferred by the nation.

Wrote and published *An American Architecture,* Horizon Press, 1955.

DALLAS THEATER CENTER, Dallas, Tex.

DECORATIVE FABRICS AND WALLPAPERS, for Schumacher & Co.

HERITAGE-HENREDON FURNITURE, three separate lines, one executed.

HOFFMAN, Max, residence (three schemes, #3 built), Manursing Island, Rye, N. Y.

KALIL, Dr. Toufic H., residence, Manchester, N. H.

LOVNESS, Don, residence, Stillwater, Minn.

PAPPAS, T. A., residence, St. Louis County, Mo.

RAYWARD, John, residence, New Canaan, Conn.

SUNDAY, Robert H., residence, Marshalltown, Iowa

TONKENS, Gerald B., residence, Cincinnati, Ohio

TRACY, W. B., residence, Seattle, Wash.

TURKEL, H., residence, Detroit, Mich.

Adelman, Benjamin, residence, Whitefish Bay, Wisc.

Barton, A. D., residence, Downer's Grove, Ill.

Blumberg, Mel, residence, Des Moines, Iowa

Boswell, William T., residence (scheme #1), Cincinnati, Ohio

Christian Science Church, Bolinas, Calif.

Coats, Robert, residence, Hillsborough, Calif.

Cooke, Andrew B., residence (Usonian block-scheme #2), Virginia Beach, Va.

Dlesk, George, residence, Manistee, Mich.

Gillin, John, residence, Hollywood, Calif.

Jankowski, Leonard, residence (scheme #1), Oakland County, Mich.

Korrick's Department Store, alterations, Phoenix, Ariz.

Lenkurt Electric Co., administration-manufacturing building, San Mateo, Calif.

Miller, Oscar, residence, Milford, Mich.

Morris, V. C., guest house, San Francisco, Calif.

"Neuroseum," hospital and clinic for the Wisconsin Neurological Society, Madison, Wisc.

Oboler, Arch, residence (scheme #2), Los Angeles, Calif.

"One Room House," (v. Bimson, 1957)

Pieper, C. R., residence, Phoenix, Ariz.

Sussman, Gerald, residence, Rye, New York

Wieland Motel, Hagerstown, Maryland

1956

Published *The Story of the Tower,* Horizon Press, 1956, upon completion of Price Tower in Bartlesville, Okla.

Honorary Degree: Doctor of Philosophy, University of Wales. Conferred by the university at Bangor.

Another year of many remarkable designs: the Greek Orthodox Church, an abstraction of Byzantine heritage; the Belmont Sports Pavilion, a vast hung canopy—the use of steel in suspension; The Mile High Illinois, a skyscraper project of 528 stories described by F.Ll.W. as "a rapier, with handle the breadth of the hand, set firmly into the ground, blade upright, as a simile. . . ."

October 17: Frank Lloyd Wright Day in Chicago, proclaimed by Mayor Daley in conjunction with an exhibition held at the Hotel Sherman to present to the public the first viewing of the designs for The Mile High Illinois.

ANNUNCIATION GREEK ORTHODOX CHURCH, for Milwaukee Hellenic Community, Milwaukee, Wisc.

AUTO SHOWROOM, for Max Hoffman, New York, N. Y.

BOTT, Frank, residence, Kansas City, Mo.

CLINIC, for Dr. Karl Kundert, San Luis Obispo, Calif.

CLINIC, for Dr. Kenneth Meyer, Dayton, Ohio

FRIEDMAN, Allan, residence, Deerfield, Ill.

MUSIC PAVILION, Taliesin West, Scottsdale, Ariz.

NOOKER, Clyde, restoration of residence (F.Ll.W. studio), Oak Park, Ill.

PRE-FAB #1, for Marshall Erdman Associates, Madison, Wisc.

SCOTT, alterations to Isabel Roberts house (v. 1908), River Forest, Ill.

SMITH, J. L., residence, Kane County, Ill.

SPENCER, Dudley W., residence, Brandywine Head, Del.

STROMQUIST, Don M., residence, Bountiful, Utah

WALTON, Dr. Robert G., residence, Modesto, Calif.

Boebel, Robert, residence, Boscobel, Wisc.

Bramlett Hotel, for Freeman Bramlett, Memphis, Tenn.

Designs for "Usonian Automatic" Houses, Frank Lloyd Wright in conjunction with his students (The Taliesin Fellowship)

"Golden Beacon," skyscraper for Chicago, Ill.

Gross, Nelson G., residence, Hackensack, N. J.

Hunt, David, residence, Scottsdale, Ariz.

Loan Office, for Gerald Tonkens, Cincinnati, Ohio

The Mile High Illinois, skyscraper, Chicago, Ill.

Mills, Bradford, residence (scheme #1), Princeton, N. J.

Morris, Mrs. V. C., "Quietwater," residence, Stinson Beach, Calif.

The New Sports Pavilion, Belmont, Long Island, N. Y.

O'Keefe, Dr. Arthur, residence, Santa Barbara, Calif.

Roberts, Jay, residence, Seattle, Wash.

Schuck, Victoria, residence, S. Hadley, Mass.

Stillman, Calvin, residence, Cornwall on Hudson, N.Y.

Vallarino, J. J., residence, Panama City, Panama

1957

Invited to Baghdad, Iraq, to design an opera house, cultural center, museum, university, and postal telegraph building. Subsequent collapse of monarchy brought all these projects to a halt. The Baghdad Opera House, however, was adapted and built for another desert region: Tempe, Arizona (v. Grady Gammage Memorial Auditorium, 1959).

Two government projects (one for Arizona and one for California) were also designed during this year. The Arizona State Capitol was never constructed, but the Marin County Government Center—the second phase—was under construction in 1966.

Wrote and published one of the most important and profound books on his work, *A Testament*, Horizon Press, 1957.

BOSWELL, William P., residence (scheme #2), Cincinnati, Ohio

CLINIC, for Dr. Herman Fasbender, Hastings, Minn.

GORDON, C. E., residence, Aurora, Ore.

JUVENILE CULTURAL STUDY CENTER, BUILDING A, for the University of Wichita, Wichita, Kans.

KINNEY, Sterling, residence, Amarillo, Tex.

MARIN COUNTY GOVERNMENT CENTER, San Raphael, Calif.

PRE-FAB #2, for Marshall Erdman Associates, Madison, Wisc.

SCHULTZ, Carl, residence, St. Joseph, Mich.

SERVICE STATION, for R. W. Lindholm, Cloquet, Minn.

TRIER, Paul J., residence, Des Moines, Iowa

WRIGHT, Duey, residence, Wausau, Wisc.

WYOMING VALLEY SCHOOL, Wyoming Valley, Wisc.

Adams, Lee, residence, St. Paul, Minn.

Ameri, Nezam, palace, Teheran, Iran (based on Millard house, 1921)

Arizona State Capitol, "Oasis," Papago Park, Phoenix, Ariz.

Baghdad Cultural Center, Baghdad, Iraq

Baghdad University, Baghdad, Iraq

Bimson, Walter, "Usonian Automatic" house, Phoenix, Ariz.

Brooks, Robert, residence, Middleton, Wisc.

Hartman, Stanley, residence, Lansing, Mich.

Hennesy, Jack P., residence (two schemes), Smoke Rise, N.J.

Herberger, Robert, residence, Maricopa County, Ariz.

Highway Motel, for Marshall Erdman Associates, Madison, Wisc.

Housing Project, for Jesse Fisher, Whiteville, N.C.

Hoyer, Carl, residence, Maricopa County, Ariz.

Juvenile Cultural Study Center, Building B, for the University of Wichita, Wichita, Kans.

Kaufmann, Edgar J., Jr., gate lodge, Bear Run, Pa.

McKinney, Darryl L., residence, Cloquet, Minn.

Miller, Arthur, residence, near Roxbury, Connecticut

Mills, Bradford, residence (scheme #2), Princeton, N.J.

Model Exhibition Houses, for U.S. Rubber Co., New York, N.Y.

Moreland, Ralph, residence, Austin, Tex.

Postal Telegraph Building, Baghdad, Iraq

Post Office, Spring Green, Wisc.

Schanbacher, G. H., store, Springfield, Ill.

Shelton, Wilton, residence, Long Island, N.Y.

Sottil, Mrs. Helen, residence, Cuernavaca, Mexico

Stracke, Victor W., residence, Appleton, Wisc.

Wedding Chapel, for Claremont Hotel, Berkeley, Calif.

Wilson, T. Henry, residence, Morgantown, N.C.

Zieger, Allen, residence, Grosse Isle, Mich.

1958

Wrote and published *The Living City,* Horizon Press, 1958, a further revision of *When Democracy Builds,* extensively edited and illustrated with new drawings.

ABLIN, Dr. George, residence, Bakersfield, Calif.

CLINIC, for Drs. Lockridge, McIntyre and Whalen, Whitefish, Mont.

OLFELT, Paul, residence, St. Louis Park, Minn.

PETERSEN, Seth, cottage, Lake Delton, Wisc.

PILGRIM CONGREGATIONAL CHURCH, (executed in part), Redding, Calif.

Clinic, for Dr. Jarvis Leuchauer, Fresno, Calif.

Colgrove, Ralph H., residence, Hamilton, Ohio

Crosby-Lambert, Lillian, residence, Colbert County, Ala.

Franklin, Jesse, residence, Louisville, Ky.

Guttierez, Dr. James F., residence, Albuquerque, New M.

Hanley, Pat, airplane hangar, Benton Harbor, Mich.

Jones Chapel ("Trinity Chapel"), University of Oklahoma, Norman, Okla.

Lagomarsino, Frank, residence, San Jose, Calif.

Libbey, Wesley, residence, Grand Rapids, Mich.

Lovness, Don, cottages, Stillwater, Minn.

Mike Todd Universal Theater, Los Angeles, Calif.

Pre-Fab #3, for Marshall Erdman Associates, Madison, Wisc.

Pre-Fab #4, for Marshall Erdman Associates, Madison, Wisc.

Spring Green Auditorium, Spring Green, Wisc.

Unity Chapel, Taliesin Valley, Spring Green, Wisc.

1959

In construction at the beginning of the year were the Solomon R. Guggenheim Museum and the Beth Sholom Synagogue.

F.Ll.W. began work on another book—a history of architecture for teenagers—to be called *The Wonderful World of Architecture,* part of a series of educational books.

The last design created by F.Ll.W. was for an EN-CLOSED GARDEN for Mrs. Frank Lloyd Wright at Taliesin, Spring Green, Wisc. Executed the following year by the members of the Taliesin Fellowship.

Frank Lloyd Wright died on April 9th, in Phoenix, Ariz.

GRADY GAMMAGE MEMORIAL AUDITORIUM, for Arizona State University, Tempe, Ariz.

RESIDENCE, Ariz. (Name and address withheld at owner's request.)

Art Gallery, for Arizona State University, Tempe, Ariz.

Donahoe, Helen C., residence, Phoenix, Ariz.

Furgatch, Harvey, residence, San Diego, Calif.

Mann, Dr. John H., residence, Putnam County, N.Y.

Penfield, Louis, residence (scheme #2), Willoughby, Ohio

Wieland, Daniel, residence, Hagerstown, Md.

Wieland, Gilbert, residence, Hagerstown, Md.

The Taliesin students who had many years of experience working under Mr. and Mrs. Wright formed the Taliesin Associated Architects; William Wesley Peters, Chief Architect. They continued and brought to completion other projects of F.Ll.W.: Solomon R. Guggenheim Museum, Beth Sholom Synagogue, Greek Orthodox Church, Building B of the Juvenile Cultural Study Center, Marin County Government Center Administration Building, Grady Gammage Memorial Auditorium and many houses. The same Taliesin-trained staff architects comprise the faculty of The Frank Lloyd Wright School of Architecture. Taliesin is now the depository of F.Ll.W.'s architectural drawings, correspondence, unpublished manuscripts and tape recordings. Mrs. Wright, president of The Frank Lloyd Wright Foundation, directs activities of the school and the firm.

BIBLIOGRAPHY

Sources of material quoted

THE FIRST YEARS

Page 19: quoted from *An Autobiography* by Frank Lloyd Wright, Longmans, Green & Co., copyright 1932 (pages 54-55).

THE BEGINNING OF WORK

13: from *An Autobiography*, 1932 (91).

THE NEW SIMPLICITY

26: from *An Autobiography*, 1932 (125).

28: from *An Autobiography*, 1932 (136-143).

A NOBLE ROOM

39: from *An Autobiography*, 1932 (153-161).

CONQUEST OF THE EARTHQUAKE

50: from *Architecture and Modern Life* by Baker Brownell and Frank Lloyd Wright, Harper and Brothers, copyright 1937 (124-139).

ARCHITECTURE AND EDUCATION

85: from *The Natural House* by Frank Lloyd Wright, Horizon Press, copyright 1954 (135-136).

ADVENTURES IN THE DESERT

103: from *An Autobiography*, 1932 (104).

FALLINGWATER

127: from *Architectural Forum*, January, 1938.

128: from *The Future of Architecture* by Frank Lloyd Wright, Horizon Press, copyright 1953 (13-14).

"IDEAS CAME TUMBLING UP AND OUT ONTO PAPER"

130: from *An Autobiography* by Frank Lloyd Wright, Duell, Sloan and Pearce, copyright 1943 (469).

ON THE ARTS

141: A statement for *Scholastic* Magazine, 1942.

142: from *A Testament* by Frank Lloyd Wright, Horizon Press, copyright 1957 (205-207).

146: from *The Natural House*, 1954 (219-221).

THE MIRACLE ON FIFTH AVENUE

163: from *Our House* by Olgivanna Lloyd Wright, Horizon Press, copyright 1959 (300-301).

165: from *The Shining Brow: Frank Lloyd Wright* by Olgivanna Lloyd Wright, Horizon Press, copyright 1960 (181, 187-188).

167: from *The Solomon R. Guggenheim Museum: Architect, Frank Lloyd Wright* published by The Solomon R. Guggenheim Foundation and Horizon Press, copyright 1960 (16-18).

All other quotations throughout the book are transcribed from unpublished manuscripts by Frank Lloyd Wright and tape-recordings of his talks, from the Taliesin archives. Information about works published since 1959 is given on the following page.

Complete listings of works by Frank Lloyd Wright published during his lifetime are included in the section "The Buildings and Projects of Frank Lloyd Wright" which begins on page 205 of this volume. Books published since 1959, containing his writings, talks or illustrations of his work, are:

1959

Frank Lloyd Wright—Drawings for a Living Architecture, published for the Bear Run Foundation and The Edgar J. Kaufmann Charitable Foundation, by Horizon Press, New York

Our House by Olgivanna Lloyd Wright, Horizon Press, New York

1960

Frank Lloyd Wright: Writings and Buildings, selected by Edgar Kaufmann, Jr. and Ben Raeburn, Horizon Press, New York

The Shining Brow—Frank Lloyd Wright by Olgivanna Lloyd Wright, Horizon Press, New York

The Solomon R. Guggenheim Museum—Architect: Frank Lloyd Wright, published by The Solomon R. Guggenheim Foundation and Horizon Press, New York

1962

The Drawings of Frank Lloyd Wright, Arthur Drexler, published for the Museum of Modern Art by Horizon Press, New York

Architecture—Man in Possession of his Earth, with a biography by Iovanna Lloyd Wright, Doubleday and Co., New York

1963

The Roots of Life by Olgivanna Lloyd Wright, Horizon Press, New York

Buildings, Plans and Designs by Frank Lloyd Wright, a new edition of the Wasmuth porfolio, with an introduction by William Wesley Peters, Horizon Press, New York

1965

The Work of Frank Lloyd Wright, a new edition of *Wendingen,* with an introduction by Olgivanna Lloyd Wright, Horizon Press, New York